HOUDINI

HOUDINI

A Pictorial Biography,
Including More Than 250 Illustrations

MILBOURNE CHRISTOPHER

GRAMERCY BOOKS
New York

For

MAURINE

who worried backstage as I swallowed needles
and brought them up threaded,
and applauded when,
though my hands were gripped by a volunteer,
I rang a dinner bell with my foot
while playing the role of Houdini
in "Magic versus The Occult"
at Alice Tully Hall, Lincoln Center, New York.

This 1998 edition is published by Gramercy Books,
a division of Random House Value Publishing, Inc.,
201 East 50th Street, New York, New York 10022,
by arrangement with the estate of Milbourne Christopher.

Gramercy Books® and design are registered trademarks of
Random House Value Publishing, Inc.

Random House
New York • Toronto • London • Sydney • Auckland
http://www.randomhouse.com/

Printed and bound in the United States of America

Library of Congress Cataloging-in-Publication Data
Christopher, Milbourne.
Houdini : a pictorial biography.
p.   cm.
Originally published: New York: Crowell, c. 1976.
Includes bibliographical references (p.) and index.
ISBN 0-517-18903-8
1. Houdini, Harry, 1874-1926.   2. Magicians—
United States—Biography.
3. Magicians—United States—Pictorial works.
4. Escape artists—United States—Biography.
5. Escape artists—United States—Pictorial works.   I. Title.
GV1545.H8C487 1998
794.8'092—dc21
[b]   97-48805
CIP

8 7 6 5 4 3 2 1

CONTENTS

HOUDINI

"King of Hand-Cuffs."

Initially Houdini challenged the police. Learning more about showmanship, he arranged for them to challenge him.

$100 REWARD
To any Sheriff, Constable,

Officer or private citizen who can produce any regulation HAND-CUFFS or LEG-SHACKLES from which **HOUDINI**, the **HAND-CUFF KING**, cannot extricate himself.

1

Master of Manacles

On the cold gray morning of March 19, 1906, Harry Houdini stripped to the skin in Cell 77 of the Boston Tombs. He sprinted upstairs to Cell 60 in the second tier, while Captain Clarence A. Swan, the prison custodian, locked the heavy iron-barred door of Cell 77, leaving Houdini's clothes behind it.

For three weeks, the stocky thirty-one-year-old vaudeville headliner had been amazing audiences at Keith's Theatre with his uncanny ability to free himself from all kinds of ingenious restraints. Nightly he accepted new challenges, releasing himself from manacles, straitjackets, strapped barrels, and nailed boxes. Now he would attempt a more sensational feat. If successful, the resulting publicity would prolong his engagement.

In Cell 60, on the second tier of the Tombs, the muscular escapologist submitted to a thorough search by prison officials in the presence of a committee from the Algonquin Club and representatives of the press. No keys were found hidden in his mouth, his ears, or any other orifices of his body. His arms were lifted; his toes pried apart; a comb was pulled through his dark, wavy hair.

Stripped to the skin and searched by prison officials, Houdini was handcuffed, leg-ironed, then locked in a cell at the Boston Tombs on March 20, 1906. Minutes later he escaped.

This diagram in the *Boston Journal* shows what happened before he scaled the prison wall, hopped into a waiting automobile, and was driven across the city to Keith's Theatre.

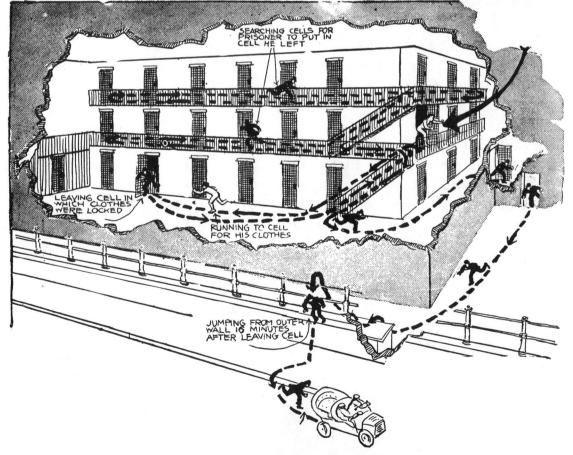

Superintendent Pierce's reaction to Houdini's jail-break at the Tombs, as pictured in the *Boston Post*.

At the request of the *Boston Globe*, the escapologist came back to the prison, and restaged for a photographer the climb over the wall.

Houdini's needle-threading mystery perplexed doctors. They examined his throat before and after the feat.

Only two possible places of concealment had been overlooked. Houdini, his blue-gray eyes sparkling, called attention to them. He lifted up first one foot, then the other, and pointed to the soles. People sometimes supposed he taped lock picks there; they were mistaken, he said.

Superintendent of Police William H. Pierce locked a pair of sturdy handcuffs on Houdini's wrists, placed leg-irons around his ankles. Pierce closed the door to Cell 60, fitted the extending hasp to a metal ring embedded in the corridor wall, then padlocked it. Photographs of the shackled nude Houdini were taken through the bars before Pierce escorted the witnesses down the stairs and across the building, making sure each door along the way was secured.

Houdini had accepted this challenge with a single proviso—no one was to watch him at work. Most of the men decided to wait with Superintendent Pierce in his office. A few thought the snow-banked Somerset Street pavement outside the prison would be a better vantage point. They proved to be right.

Sixteen minutes after Houdini was incarcerated, they saw him, fully clothed, scale the outer wall of the prison yard, leap over the iron railing, and jump down. He hopped into a waiting car beside the driver. As the automobile roared off toward the center of the city, Houdini leaned out and waved.

This news produced pandemonium in the prison. The observers reported that the door to Cell 77 had been left ajar. Cell 60 was open, too, and empty except for the manacles heaped on the floor. The doors to five other

A challenge escape from a coffin at the Athletic Club in Boston added tension to his performance.

cells had been unlocked. Houdini later explained he had planned to switch prisoners from one cubicle to another, until he discovered he was the sole occupant of the tiers.

A massive barrier, equipped with an intricate bolting device, at the entrance to the passageway through which inmates were taken to the law courts, and another heavy portal midway along this passage had been breached. Footprints in the snow outside indicated the course Houdini had taken as he dashed to the outer wall.

The Boston jailbreak is not an isolated example of Houdini's ingenuity; he escaped from many similar strongholds in various parts of the world. His ability to release himself from almost every conceivable type of restraint made him a legend in his own time. Movies, stage productions, television specials, and books have perpetuated his fame. His fictional encounters with Harry K. Thaw, the murderer of architect Stanford White, with socialite Mrs. Stuyvesant Fish, and with Archduke Franz Ferdinand of Austria enlivened E. L. Doctorow's recent best-selling novel *Ragtime*.

Alert newsmen were intrigued when they heard that on the one hundredth anniversary of Houdini's birth, in the spring of 1974, a safe-deposit box would be opened in New York City by his lawyer to reveal the escapologist's secrets.

The London *Daily Mirror*, French, German, and Australian papers, even Russia's *Pravda* sought further details. When they came to me, as author of a full-length biography, *Houdini: The Untold Story*, I explained that

Houdini offered $1000 to anyone who could find any evidence of trickery
in this padlocked and roped hamper, from which he released himself.

For Houdini,
  The great Handcuff King,
Who wriggles to freedom
From any old thing.

Only one performer was mentioned by name in the souvenir ABC booklet presented to patrons of Keith's Theatre in Boston.

HOUDINI can get away from these handcuffs, but you can't get away from these facts: THE LARGEST CROWDS, THE BEST MEATS, THE LOWEST PRICES.
at the
Central Market

Look at these prices for Saturday:

Butterine, 10 pounds for	$1 00
Pork Loins	5¼c
Spare Ribs	4½c
Pork Butts	5½c
California Hams	4¾c
Leaf Lard, 17 pounds for	$1 00
Pork Chops, 4 pounds for	25c
Bacon	8½c
Kettle Rendered Lard, 4 pounds for	25c
Mutton	3½c
Rib Roast	8c
Good Steak, 3 pounds for	25c
Round Steak	10c
Sirloin Steak	12c
Hamburger	7½c

Poultry at Lowest Prices.
Phone 1796.   16th and Capitol Ave.

As early as 1899, Houdini was featured in advertisements designed to catch the eyes of newspaper readers in American cities.

Houdini, his wife, and their largest and most applauded feat, Metamorphosis—a substitution illusion.

Left and *below left:* Bound to a steel girder on the tower of an unfinished building in midtown New York, Houdini struggled to free himself.

Above right and *right:* Completing the task, he ran to the photographer, and told him to take a picture of the spectators on the streets below.

him to add his signature. As soon as Dunninger had complied, Houdini again took the book and wrote the word "witness" under Dunninger's name. "Making it appear," Dunninger complained as he recalled the episode, "that I merely authenticated his autograph."

Houdini's younger brother Theo, who performed as Hardeen, idolized him; his assistants admired him. Hardeen named a son Harry Houdini, as did Franz Kukol, the escapologist's chief aide.

Rival escape artists had reason to fear Houdini. He interrupted the acts of those who advertised they were equal or superior to him, publicly shaming them by daring them to extricate themselves from standard but complex manacles. He denounced "jail breakers" who had to bribe prison guards to get out, lambasting them in print at every opportunity.

Dai Vernon, an expert sleight-of-hand performer, tells a story related to him by Hardeen. Enraged by a circus escapologist who claimed to be greater, though he would never meet a legitimate challenge, Houdini set fire to the structure where the show was being exhibited. Afterward, he said he regretted this rash act, "Innocent jungle beasts might have been destroyed." No evidence to confirm this anecdote has been found, but the tale symbolizes the intense antagonism Houdini felt for his rivals.

Houdini and his wife were both fond of animals. He taught Bobby—one of their several pet dogs—to release his paws from a pair of miniature handcuffs. He noted in a letter how his wife grieved when her favorite canary died.

Aware of the unpredictable responses of caged creatures, Houdini was amazed to read that J. B. Bardelle, one of his rivals in Britain, was featuring an escape more dangerous than any he had attempted himself. Bardelle, manacled hand and foot, freed himself in a cage housing five wolves, two hyenas, and three bears. At least, he did until one of the wolves sprang at him and fastened its teeth in his neck. Quick action by assistants saved Bardelle's life. They prodded the wolf with long poles through the bars until it released its grip, then rescued the wounded, terrified performer.

Though daring, Houdini never took unnecessary risks. He would not jump, handcuffed, from a bridge until he had satisfied himself that the water below was sufficiently deep and that there was no hazardous obstacle lurking beneath the surface. He never accepted a challenge to escape from a nailed box, riveted cylinder, sealed coffin, or liquid-filled, padlocked can until he had examined the restraint and worked out a sure-fire release.

As a young man, Houdini once permitted a conniving Chicago policeman to handcuff him in a dime museum. Before the confrontation, the officer jammed a metal slug deep into one of the locks. The cuff could not be removed without breaking it. Thereafter Houdini specified all challenge manacles must be in perfect working condition and accompanied by a key. After testing the lock by opening and closing it, he would return the key and extend his wrists for shackling.

All the initial odds were against Houdini's success. Born Ehrich Weiss (Erik Weisz in the Hungarian spelling) on March 24, 1874, in Budapest, he crossed the Atlantic for the first time as an infant in the arms of his mother, Cecilia. His immigrant father, Mayer Samuel Weiss, earned $750 a year as the first rabbi in Appleton, Wisconsin. With four sons born in Hungary—Herman (Armin), Nathan, William, and Ehrich—and two more, Theodore and Leopold, born in Wisconsin, the bearded scholar found it hard to provide for his family. After he lost his Appleton post, the Weisses moved to nearby Milwaukee, where he earned even less as a teacher of the Torah.

Houdini later said he made his first professional appearance as a trapeze performer with Jack Hoeffler's five-cent circus in Appleton. Actually the Weisses were living in Milwaukee then; the "five-cent circus" had been staged by young Jack in the Hoeffler backyard.

Ehrich ran away from home at the age of twelve, hoping to be able to contribute more to the family income than he had been doing by shining shoes and selling newspapers. The larger income failed to materialize, and he joined his father, who had traveled east in search of a better paying position, in New York City. Between them, they scrimped and saved until they could bring Cecilia and the younger children east. Gladys, the Weisses' only daughter, was born in New York.

The best job Ehrich could get was as an assistant cutter in a necktie factory on lower Broadway. Now in his early teens, he was an avid reader, and he developed his body as well as his mind by being a medal-winning member of two neighborhood track teams. He also learned how to swim and dive in the murky waters of the East River, a few blocks away from the Weiss home on East 69th Street.

Ehrich had seen his first magic show in Milwaukee. Dr. H. S. Lynn, a British showman, had been popular at Egyptian Hall in London; he featured a vivisection illusion—cutting off an assistant's arm, leg, and head, and then restoring them. A first-rate conjurer, Lynn accompanied his deceptions with a flow of humorous comments. In later years, Houdini vividly recalled this performance. But young Ehrich learned his first trick—the vanishing and reappearing quarter—in New York. There he also read the book that was to change his life: *Memoirs of Robert-Houdin*. Accounts of the feats Robert-Houdin presented at his theatre in Paris, the stories of his performance for Queen Victoria in England and of his exciting mission to North Africa, intrigued the young tie-cutter. Robert-Houdin had made a rebellion vanish by

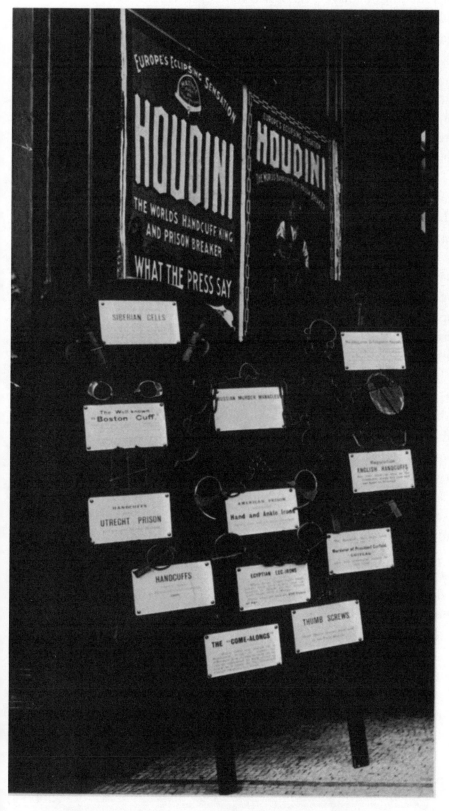

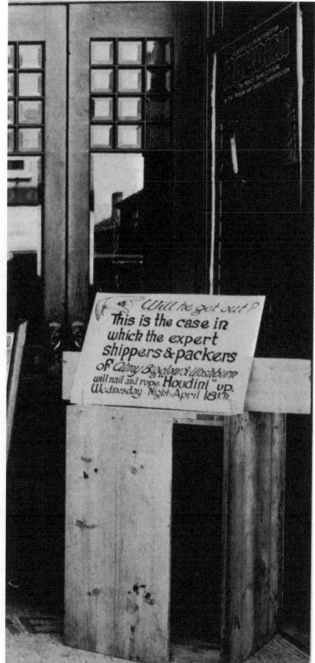

A packing crate from which Houdini would release himself, after having been nailed inside, was put on display in the theatre lobby.

Official prison manacles from Europe and Asia, as well as America, intrigued theatre-goers on their way to see challenges met on stage.

this, like many other tales about Houdini, was a myth. My friend, the late B. M. L. Ernst, Houdini's lawyer, had long ago assured me that stories of such a cache of secrets were unfounded.

I traced the most persistent rumor to a statement made in October 1936 by Edward Saint, Mrs. Houdini's manager. Saint had told reporters that the decorations Houdini had received from European royalty, important family documents, and a large amount of cash had not been found by his widow. He surmised that this material had been placed in a box in a Manhattan bank.

Imaginative writers said a manuscript explaining Houdini's methods was enclosed in the mythical container. *Reader's Digest* did not check the facts; it simply reprinted one of these articles and gave wide circulation to the unsubstantiated claim.

Norman Bigelow, a New England locksmith, who presents a show billed as "Houdini Reincarnated," told a similarly strange tale in 1975. He said he had broken a Houdini code and learned the secrets were hidden in the monument marking the master mystifier's grave at Machpelah Cemetery in Queens, New York. Vandals, perhaps thinking this information was inside the bust of Houdini on the exedra, smashed the head. It, like the rest of the marker, had been chiseled from solid marble. The Society of American Magicians has since replaced the desecrated sculpture.

Houdini's *real* secrets were his dynamic showmanship and his determination to succeed—not the methods he used for release from constraints. He himself described how he was able to open manacles, escape from ropes, and free himself from straitjackets and other restraints in books and magazine articles, and in unpublished manuscripts now in the Christopher Collection. Other escape artists have employed the same procedures. Only Houdini presented the feats so dramatically that he became a folk hero.

Houdini has other claims to fame. A master magician, as well as a master escapologist, he produced eagles, caused live elephants to disappear. He made the first successful airplane flight in Australia in 1910. A star of the silent films, he wrote and produced his own feature pictures. A relentless exposer of fraud, he more than any psychical researcher of his era alerted the public to the deceptions practiced by supposed mediums in darkened rooms.

Charlatans detested Houdini, but to his wife he was an attentive, loving companion who never forgot a birthday or wedding anniversary. Joseph Dunninger, a younger magician, thought Houdini overrated as a conjurer, though a magnificent showman. Perhaps Dunninger was rankled by the memory of an incident that occurred backstage at the New York Hippodrome: A stranger asked Houdini to autograph one of his books. After Houdini inscribed the flyleaf, the visitor recognized Dunninger and invited

ALHAMBRA THEATRE

General Manager - - **C. DUNDAS SLATER**

TO-NIGHT.

Mr. HARRY

HOUDINI

The World's Greatest Mystifier

AND

KING OF HANDCUFFS.

Front cover of four-page brochure distributed along with the theatre
program to patrons of the London Alhambra Theatre in 1900.

Letters of Verification from the American Police Officials that
HOUDINI is the "KING OF HANDCUFFS."

HEADQUARTERS OF POLICE DEPARTMENT, PROVIDENCE, R.I.,
Jan. 26th, 1900.

This is to certify that HARRY HOUDINI gave a private exhibition at Police Headquarters in the Detective Bureau Jan. 26th, 1900. Prior to his exhibition he was stripped completely nude, was examined by a local physician, and it was conclusive that he had nothing upon his person. His mouth was sealed with court plaster by the physician, and he was then shackled hands and feet, the several ankle and handcuffs being joined by the other shackles. It required nine minutes to shackle him, and he removed and unlocked all the irons in two minutes and forty-one seconds in a most remarkable manner.

Respectfully,   WILLIAM G. BAKER, *Mayor.*
JAMES A. GEORGE, *Secretary to Mayor.*
P. EGAN, *Deputy Chief of Police.*
S. L. W. MERRILL, *Detective.*
P. PARKER, *Capt. Detective Bureau.*
WILLIAM GARDINER, *Clerk of Police.*

OFFICE OF CHIEF OF POLICE, MEMPHIS, TENN.,
Oct. 24th, 1899.

To whom it may concern : This to certify that Mr. HARRY HOUDINI gave an exhibition at the Central Police Station in this city to-day, in the presence of about twenty-five officers, and we can highly endorse him as a wonder in his line. We placed seven pairs of handcuffs on him at one time and in every manner possible, and he released himself in less than ten minutes. He was previously stripped naked and searched.

JEROME E. RICHARDS, *Chief of Police.*
W. S. LAWLESS, *Detective.*
J. A. PERKINS, *Detective.*
HAYET CHILES, *Detective.*
E. BUTTINGHOUS, *Detective.*

HEADQUARTERS OF POLICE DEPARTMENT, NASHVILLE, TENN.,
Nov. 7th, 1899.

To whom it may concern :—This is to certify that Mr. HARRY HOUDINI gave an exhibition in the Nashville police station this afternoon of his method of escaping out of handcuffs. He stripped naked, was handcuffed by a member of the detective force, his mouth was sealed with court plaster, all in the room where the Chief of Police, Chief of Detectives, and a number of officers of the force were present. He stripped behind an improvised curtain and in a few moments appeared, entirely free from his shackles. He also gave a marvellous exhibition of the manipulation of playing cards.

HENRY CURRAN, *Chief of Police.*
M. A. MARSHALL, *Chief of Detectives.*
J. E. FOGARTY, *City Detective.*

METROPOLITAN POLICE DEPARTMENT, KANSAS CITY, MO.,
OFFICE OF CHIEF OF POLICE, KANSAS CITY, MO., *April 11th*, 1899.

To whom this may concern : — This is to certify that HARRY HOUDINI gave an exhibition at my office in Central Police station to several officers and newspaper men in the way of "beating" handcuffs. He is certainly a wonder. I put several pairs of different makes on him and sent him into a room alone. He returned in a few minutes with them all off.

Yours truly,
JOHN HALPIN, *Inspector of Detectives.*

HEADQUARTERS OF CHIEF OF POLICE, SAN FRANCISCO, CAL.

We, the undersigned, hereby certify that we witnessed an exhibition given by Prof. H. HOUDINI, on the evening of July 13th, 1899, in the chamber of the detective force at the head-

Inside two pages of brochure distributed to patrons of the London Alhambra Theatre in 1900.

HOUDINI is the "KING OF HANDCUFFS."

quarters of the San Francisco Police Department. HOUDINI had never been in these rooms before. We saw him stripped absolutely naked. Police-Surgeon R. E. Hartley and two assistants submitted the naked conjuror to a searching examination for concealed keys and other instruments, searching from between toes to tips of hair, the eyes, nose, ears and mouth thoroughly examined, and the mouth sealed up by Surgeon Hartley with adhesive plaster, marked so as to make it impossible to remove or tamper with it. HOUDINI was then shackled hands and feet, his hands afterwards being locked to the irons imprisoning his feet. The cuffs were supplied by officers and detectives present, ten pairs were used of nine different styles. HOUDINI was then carried into a closet into which he had never been, no one knew it was to be used, as it was decided upon after he was secured and mouth sealed, he having no choice in the matter. It was searched before and after, but in less than ten minutes he walked out freed, and the cuffs interlocked, proved he had not slipped them. He was then secured in an insane belt. Next the straight jacket, procured from the Insane Asylum, was locked and laced on HOUDINI by Superintendent of the insane department, James Nolan, but he succeeded in again escaping without damaging locks, straps or straight jacket. To the truth of the above we voluntarily subscribe our names this 13th day of July, 1899.

M. J. CONVOY, *Sergt. Police.*
P. SULLIVAN, G. E. MADDEN, G. W. MCMALLORY, DAVID SULLIVAN, *Police Officers.*
THOS. P. ELLIS, S. HOOVEY, J. T. CROSETT, R. M. SILVEY, *Detectives.*
Dr. R. E. HARTLEY, *Police Surgeon* (examined HOUDINI.
ED. M. JONES, *D.D.S.*
E. M. EAGAN, THOS. B. GIBSON, H. C. REYNOLDS, T. DILLON, *Detective P.D.*
JAMES NOLAN, *Supt. Insane Ward.*

DETECTIVE SERVICE, BUREAU OF POLICE, PHILADELPHIA, PA., *Feb. 9th, 1900.*

This is to certify that HARRY HOUDINI was stripped stark naked, his mouth sealed up, and he was thoroughly searched by Dr. Anthony J. Hill, to prove he had nothing concealed on his person in the shape of keys, wires, springs, or lock-picks. His hands were cuffed behind his back, and leg-irons placed on his ankles by Captain Peter Miller, who used his own private irons. HOUDINI assumed a stooping position, and was successful in releasing himself from all fetters locked upon him. All of which was done in our presence.

P. MILLER, *Captain o Detectives.*
J. WARREN DELANEY.
R. D. CAMERON.

OFFICE OF CHIEF OF POLICE, LOS ANGELES, CAL., *June 24th, 1899.*

To whom it may concern:—Professor HARRY HOUDINI gave an exhibition of his skill as "King of Handcuffs" in the Assembly Rooms of the Department. He was securely cuffed with four pairs of cuffs (different varieties), shackles placed on his legs, and also an Oregon boot. These were placed on him in the presence of my officers and many spectators. He was carried to an adjoining room, and in less than four minutes appeared, entirely released, with the cuffs fastened together in such a manner that it showed beyond a doubt that they had all been unlocked.

Very respectfully,
J. M. GLASS,
Chief of Police.

Letters of Verification from the American Police Officials that
HOUDINI is the "KING OF HANDCUFFS."

CITY OF CINCINNATI, DEPARTMENT OF POLICE,
CINCINNATI, O., *Dec. 8th*, 1899.

To whom it may concern:—This is to certify that HARRY HOUDINI, the "King of Handcuffs," exhibited in the presence of about fifteen gentlemen his ability to release himself from handcuff and ankle irons. There were two pairs of pinkerton handcuffs placed upon his wrists, and one pair of ankle irons with a 12-inch chain. The cuffs and irons were fastened together with a pair of Pinkerton's handcuffs.

These cuffs and irons were fastened upon his wrists and ankles by Luke Drout, acting superintendent of police, and R. A. Crawford, Acting chief of detectives, and it took HOUDINI less than three minutes to extricate himself from these cuffs and irons. He did not have a particle of clothing on his body. His mouth was firmly closed with adhesive plaster and marked, so that he could not have taken it off without our knowledge. He therefore could have had nothing concealed about his person. His hair, ears, mouth and hands were examined carefully and nothing could be found that he could make use of.

LUKE DROUT, *Acting Supt. Police.*
RALPH A. CRAWFORD, *Acting Chief of Detectives.*
J. DRAPER, *Sec. Supt. of Police.*

DEPARTMENT OF POLICE, OMAHA, NEBRASKA.
April, 1899.

To Whom it may Concern:—I take great pleasure in commenting on the excellent exhibition given the police department of this city by Prof. HARRY HOUDINI, who appeared at police headquarters last evening before the entire police department of Omaha, and was shackled and handcuffed to the extent of five pairs of handcuffs of different styles, and one pair of leg irons, the same being placed on him in such a manner as to absolutely prevent him using any keys or other instruments of a like nature to effect his release. It took certain members of the department a little better than twelve minutes to shackle Prof. HOUDINI as described; he left the room, and in less than four minutes returned completely liberated. At the time of his return the shackles were locked, and in such a state that it took fully five minutes to separate them by officers well acquainted with the workings of shackles and handcuffs. The exhibition was marvellous, and cannot help but be of interest to any police official.

Respectfully yours,
J. J. DONOHUE,
Acting Chief of Police.

**POSITIVELY
The only Person
in the World that
Escapes out of all
Handcuffs,
Leg Shackles,
Belts, and
Straight Jackets,
without using
Keys, Springs,
or Concealed
Accessories.**

**Allows the Police
to Iron him in
every conceivable
Position, and with
as many Cuffs
as they wish.**

HOUDINI
**Does not Slip his Hands or Feet, but Opens each
Lock without Breaking or Injuring it in any way.
Defies Duplication, Explanation, or Imitation.**

Last page of brochure distributed to patrons of the London Alhambra Theatre in 1900.

outconjuring the Marabouts, a fanatical sect that had advised the Algerian chieftains to sever their ties with France. Ehrich (by then called Harry) decided to take a name similar to his idol's—Houdini—and, at the age of seventeen, set out to be a magician himself.

Houdini's first partner, Jack Hayman (Hyman), left his bench at the necktie factory to join the act. More interested in other phases of show business, Hayman soon resigned as one of the "Brothers Houdini"; he was replaced by Theo, Houdini's younger brother. Theo, in turn, was supplanted by Bess—Wilhelmina Beatrice Rahner—the dark-haired, slightly built girl whom Houdini met and married when he was twenty. Bess's Roman Catholic mother did not approve of her daughter's union with the son of a rabbi; Cecilia Weiss, on the other hand, welcomed the couple to her home.

Working in dime museums, with a circus, a medicine show, and at one time with an older magician, playing in occasional halls and theatres as far west as Kansas and as far north as Nova Scotia, the Houdinis rarely made more than twenty or thirty dollars a week. Even so, Houdini always managed to send a portion of his salary to his mother. During one bleak period, he posed briefly as a medium. Adept at sleight of hand, personable, and constantly improving as a showman, he finally broke through on the big-time vaudeville circuits not as a magician but as an escape artist. Martin Beck of the Orpheum vaudeville circuit, one of the shrewdest bookers of the period, saw Houdini perform in St. Paul, Minnesota. When Houdini successfully escaped from a pair of handcuffs provided by Beck, he convinced him that he could release himself from any sort of manacles. Beck advised him to eliminate magic from his act and to specialize in escapes. Through arduous study during the lean years, Houdini had learned how to open shackles in ways audiences never suspected. He was thus fully prepared for the first date Beck arranged for him in Omaha, Nebraska, in the spring of 1899. Houdini's challenge releases on the Orpheum circuit in the west created a sensation. Within a few months his exploits as a headliner had brought him more money than he had ever dreamed of.

After successfully topping Keith theatre bills in the east, Houdini and his wife sailed for England in May 1900. While abroad, he became the strongest attraction in international vaudeville. Advertising heavily in theatrical journals, he also mailed lengthy accounts of his exploits to American publications.

Before he opened in Boston in 1906, exciting stories in the press had whetted public interest. Houdini had freed himself from a locked, metallined Siberian prison van in Moscow! Challenged in London by the *Daily Illustrated Mirror*, he had slipped free from formidable handcuffs with six locks

Harry and Bess Houdini awaiting an early morning train in a London railroad station, with two British assistants and many pieces of baggage.

Houdini bought an automobile in England. Clad in motoring regalia of the time, he took his wife and Martin Beck, his American manager, out for a drive.

A medal-winning athlete as a young man, Houdini exercised daily throughout his career. Physical fitness was essential for his strenuous feats.

and nine sets of tumblers in each manacle! He escaped from the death-row cell of the federal prison in Washington where Charles Guiteau, the assassin of President James A. Garfield, had been incarcerated before being taken to the gallows!

Lithographs showing the "World's Handcuff King and Only Prison Breaker" in action were posted throughout the city. In the lobby of Keith's theatre stood a heart-shaped display board on which were displayed some of the shackles he had mastered.

On the night of February 27 Houdini, in evening clothes, walked quickly to the footlights. Anyone, he stated, could bring challenge manacles to the stage. Half a dozen men came forward. Houdini directed them to seats on the stage, then went from one to another scrutinizing the "prison jewelry" they held, testing each lock.

At his suggestion, three pairs of the handcuffs were fastened on his wrists and arms; his ankles were locked in leg-irons. He bent over so a fifth pair could be closed around the metal links between his hands and his feet.

Two uniformed assistants carried Houdini center stage to a cloth-sided cabinet, put him on the floor within it, then closed the front curtains. A third assistant immediately held up a stopwatch and pressed the activating button. Spectators throughout the theatre took out their own timepieces. One minute passed; two minutes, three minutes, four. Houdini burst through the curtains. His evening clothes were rumpled; beads of perspiration rolled down his cheeks; but he was free.

The second feat, by contrast, seemed lightning fast. A challenger secured his wrists with a single pair of shackles behind his back. Assistants shoved the cabinet forward, so Houdini could be seen from the front but not from the sides. He grimaced, strained, then extended his arms. The cuffs were still locked, but they were no longer on his wrists. He displayed them with one hand, smiled, and took a bow.

Another change of pace came as Houdini told of having been slandered by a German policeman, Werner Graff, who had charged that Houdini could not escape from all official restraints as he had advertised. Houdini sued Graff for libel. When the case was tried in Cologne in February 1902, Houdini won. Graff appealed; Houdini won again. Graff took the case to the highest court in Germany. There, the following July, Houdini won once more; Graff was fined and ordered to pay for a printed apology. In the lower court, at the judge's insistence, Houdini had escaped from a transport chain, used instead of handcuffs in Germany when a prisoner was conveyed from one jail to another. This was the first time he had ever effected such a release in full view. He would now show the audience what occurred.

Two volunteers bound his wrists with a chain. Drawing it tight, forcing the links into his flesh, they fastened it with a padlock. Houdini walked forward to the footlights, displaying the chain on his wrists to the audience. He then stepped back and began to struggle, tugging, pulling, using his teeth, as he tried to gain slack. Suddenly he spun around. The turning masked the final movement; the chain, still padlocked, was now off. He let it clatter to the floor of the stage.

Houdini's opening night act ended with Metamorphosis, his first big stage feat. It was as effective in Boston as it had been years before in New York. His hands were tied behind his back with a length of tape. Clutching a coat borrowed from a member of the audience, he darted into the cabinet. Assistants closed the front curtains; then almost immediately opened them again. Houdini came forward wearing the borrowed coat, though his hands were still secured.

In the second phase of this feat, Houdini, still bound and wearing the borrowed coat, was tied in a sack, then locked in a trunk. A heavy rope was knotted around it. Assistants pulled the open cabinet forward until it covered the trunk. Bess Houdini entered the cabinet, drew the curtains together; only her head could be seen. She counted, "One, two, three." On the count of three, Houdini's head appeared where Bess's had been. He threw open the curtains, and with the aid of his assistants, shoved the cabinet back, untied the rope, and unlocked the trunk. Inside, tied in the sack, wearing the oversized borrowed coat, with her hands bound with tape as her husband's had been, was Mrs. Houdini.

Metamorphosis, the *Boston Post* critic reported, "is done so neatly, so rapidly, and the illusion is so complete, that the house bursts into a torrent of applause. . . . The celerity with which the act moves counts toward its success, but his whole turn is a marvelous exhibition that will lead to endless discussion."

While this was the basic Houdini act, the great escapologist varied it constantly to meet challenges. One night four sailors roped him to a chair. He rocked the chair from side to side until it toppled over. Squirming and straining, he kicked off his shoes and eventually slipped clear of the bonds. Another evening, after being strapped in a straitjacket, he dropped to the floor, rolling and tossing "like a cat in a bag" until he wrenched the leather and canvas restraint up, over his head, and off.

A skeptical dealer in police supplies challenged Houdini to escape from his whole stock of manacles. This took time, but he successfully met the dare. A Dorchester doctor with an antique set of irons succeeded, despite Houdini's objections, in fastening them behind his back, rather than in front. This was the sort of situation that made the Houdini act so intriguing. Before entering the cabinet, Houdini pushed his linked hands down to his

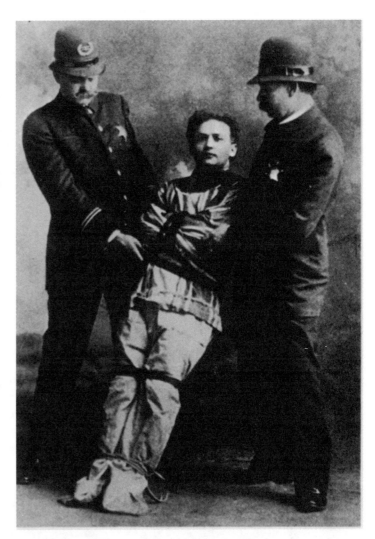

Washington, D.C., policemen shackled, leg-ironed, and chained Houdini. After he released himself, they strapped and tied his legs in a bag, then fastened him in a straitjacket. Again he freed himself.

When European escape artists capitalized on Houdini's success, Harry brought his brother, Theo, across the ocean to perform as Hardeen. Hardeen later headlined in American vaudeville.

buttocks. Then, sitting on the floor, with considerable exertion, he pulled his legs through the loop made by his shackled hands, and brought the irons to the front of his body. This prodigious feat of contortion in full view generated as much applause as the covered release that followed it.

During the record-shattering seven-week engagement in Boston, Houdini penetrated—without leaving behind clues to his procedures—a nailed packing crate and an iron-bound, rectangular hamper made by the Wakefield Rattan Company. Once he was inside the hamper, the top was closed, fastened with five padlocks and sealed with signed paper disks. Then the hamper was wound and secured with ropes and chains. Still Houdini escaped.

The *Boston American* invited readers to contribute limericks celebrating the accomplishments of the man who performed astonishing feats on the stage and who had broken out of a cell in the Tombs. Three of those submitted follow:

> Houdini is surely a wizard,
> He "contorts" like a snake or a lizard;
>   How he clothing resumes,
>   Then escapes from the "Tombs,"
> Is exactly what sticks in the gizzard.

> Have you heard of Houdini, at Keith's
> The eighth wonder who comes from the East?
>   Steel doors, locks and chains,
>   Are dead easy, he claims:
> If you doubt it, just ask the police.

Other supporting performers were on the bill with Houdini in Poplar, England. There was no doubt, however, that he was the major attraction.

The three men wearing derbies are Houdini assistants: James Collins, James Vickery, and Louis Goldsmith. They accompanied his baggage from the Croydon railroad terminal to the Empire Theatre stage door.

Houdini, you've won every bet,
Whether handcuffs, or hamper, or net:
    Now you must know a way,
    So tell us pray,
How a poor man can get out of debt.

For a special Houdini Day at the theatre, souvenir pictures were distributed, and an enormous floral display in the shape of a pair of handcuffs was brought to the stage by the house manager. B. F. Keith presented Houdini with a thousand-dollar Tiffany watch as a token of his appreciation.

This watch, editor Sime Silverman noted years later in *Variety*, the leading American vaudeville weekly, cost Houdini far more than the thousand dollars Keith paid for it. Houdini was so moved by what seemed to be Keith's very generous gesture that he decided not to ask for the hefty boost in salary he deserved. Houdini never fully realized his worth as an attraction, Silverman continued. Oscar S. Teale, a former president of the Society of American Magicians who for several years was on Houdini's staff as a research assistant and part-time secretary, agreed with this view.

Bored by business details, Houdini occupied his spare time with matters of more importance to him. He collected data on the early history of magic and assembled remarkable collections on conjuring, the theatre, and crime.

WHERE THE POSSIBILITY CEASES, THE IMPOSSIBILITY COMMENCES!

HARRY HOUDINI

"KING OF HANDCUFFS."

POSITIVELY

The only Conjurer in the WORLD

That Escapes out of all Handcuffs, Leg Shackles, Insane Belts and Strait-Jackets, after being STRIPPED STARK NAKED, mouth sealed up, and thoroughly searched from head to foot, proving he carries no Keys, Springs, Wires or concealed accessories.

DEFIES

Duplication, Explanation, Imitation or Contradiction.

Allowing the Police to Iron Him in every conceivable position, and with as many cuffs as they wish—The more the merrier.

Bringing out all the Cuffs, interlocked, proving he does not slip his hands or feet.

UNDER THE MANAGEMENT OF

Martin Beck,

Ashland Building, Chicago, Ill.

Now Playing a Featured

TOP LINER ENGAGEMENT

ON THE KEITH CIRCUIT.

Baffled the Police in New York City as well as out West.

As soon as he could pay for them, Houdini took full-page advertisements in theatrical papers.

Hardeen and Houdini, friendly rivals, pose for a picture in Joplin, Missouri.

Houdini published his first book, *The Right Way to Do Wrong. An Exposé of Successful Criminals*, during the 1906 engagement in Boston. It revealed the ruses of thieves, confidence men, and mediums. He also made plans for a periodical, *Conjurers' Monthly Magazine*, which he edited for two years. In its pages, prepared in his dressing rooms on the road, he printed news from correspondents in Vienna, London, Moscow, and a number of American cities. Most of the space was devoted to his own writing—illustrated accounts of earlier wonder-workers, articles on methods for handcuff escapes and jail releases, and attacks on his rivals. He slashed at Will Goldston, the editor of *The Magician* in Britain, and at Dr. A. M. Wilson, publisher of the American *Sphinx*. Despite these denunciations, Goldston and Wilson later became two of Houdini's most ardent supporters.

Dr. Walter Franklin Prince, a fellow member of the *Scientific American* committee investigating psychical phenomena, noted Houdini's remarkable skill in human relations. He "could make a man white in the face with rage by accusing that man of improper or grossly plundering conduct, and within ten minutes soothe the man's plumage and be in pleasant conversation with him."

My friend, the late John Mulholland, recalled an example of this side of Houdini's character. John, who was to become a famous conjurer himself, met the older man in New York. He frequently visited Houdini's home on

West 113th Street. Mulholland, like Houdini, was interested in learning more about the past history of magic. One afternoon he brought an unusual book with him. Houdini opened it to a page illustrated with the picture of a peacock. Until then gracious, Houdini suddenly exploded. Peacocks, he roared, were unlucky. He ordered John out of the house.

A few days later, a package arrived in the mail containing a set of scarce books that Mulholland had been searching for without much hope of success. When he met Houdini, Houdini asked if he had received the gift. John said there had been no indication of the sender on the parcel. Houdini shook his head and sighed: "Who else would send you such a valuable present?"

At times, Houdini could be very compassionate. Dr. Prince was once with him backstage when an elderly woman "persisted in telling him a long and tedious string of domestic concerns, and I thought from his patience and sympathy that they must be old friends." After she left, Houdini said he had never met her before.

Though he never lacked stamina for his rigorous stage demonstrations, Houdini seldom slept more than five hours a night. The extra period of wakefulness was not wasted. He jotted down ideas for tricks he would like to perform, outlines for future books, plots for possible movie scenarios, and tried to catch up on his extensive correspondence. Some letters were answered with a "Houdinigram." Similar in appearance to a Western Union form, this had his likeness and a printed apology for brevity at the top, and just enough space for a short reply at the bottom.

While entries in the diaries Houdini kept were often sparse and seldom mentioned his famous escapes, scrapbooks filled with clippings covered these events in detail.

His idea of misery, Houdini told an interviewer from *Picture Plays* magazine, was "arriving in a town at midnight on a drizzly, wet, foggy night and finding all the hotels full up." He felt at his worst on the ocean: "Once while sailing round the world at a longitude of eighty degrees, we had two Tuesdays in one week and no Wednesday, which meant losing a Christmas, and I was seasick at the time." A sentimentalist, he singled out "Auld Lang Syne" as his favorite song; his greatest ambition was "to live a life and die being worthy of the mother who bore me."

Family ties were stronger in Houdini's time than they are today. Even so, his deep affection for the understanding mother who encouraged his early efforts as a magician and shared his tribulations and triumphs puzzled less emotional people. He collapsed in the vestibule of Copenhagen's Cirkus Beketow in 1913 when he received the cablegram telling him of her death. Grief-stricken, he canceled his engagement in Denmark and returned to

New York to supervise the funeral, delayed despite Jewish tradition by his desire to see her face once again before she was buried.

He would have welcomed the slightest confirmable sign that his beloved mother was still with him in spirit. Inane messages, purporting to be from her, intensified his crusade against psychic fraud. The psychics his friend Sir Arthur Conan Doyle recommended in England and the United States were as disappointing as those he had investigated on his own.

The creator of Sherlock Holmes sat in a darkened Atlantic City hotel room with Houdini one summer afternoon while Lady Doyle filled several pages with words allegedly transmitted by Cecilia Weiss through her hand. Houdini's mother had always written to him in German; the message came through in English, a language she had never mastered. A Christian cross was inscribed at the top of the first page—an unlikely emblem, he noted, to be drawn by the wife of a rabbi.

Houdini failed to hail this communication as authentic, and Sir Arthur severed their friendship. Fulton Oursler, an author, editor, and amateur conjurer, knew both men. They were, he said, "self-contradictory symbols." Doyle expressed a keen, analytical sense of reasoning in his stories about the Baker Street detective; but ignoring any scientific assessment of séances, he became "the St. Paul of spiritualists." Houdini, to Oursler, seemed "a contradiction without parallel . . . at once the popular image for mysticism and for skepticism." His seemingly miraculous feats awed the public, but he denied having supernormal powers and proclaimed he could reproduce any "psychic marvel" by natural means.

"Houdini knew everything and understood nothing; Doyle knew nothing and understood everything," Oursler concluded.

Oursler, intent on provocative phrases, missed the point of Houdini's campaign against the occultists. As a specialist in trickery, he could detect fraud. Though it was not to his advantage as a legitimate performer of mysteries, he purposely revealed techniques gullible believers never suspected. Houdini knew how the bereaved were cheated; he sought to enlighten them.

Edmund Wilson, the eminent literary critic, was more perceptive than Oursler. He, too, had studied magic as an avocation. Wilson says in *The Shores of Light* that during the final years, as Houdini crusaded against fraudulent psychics, he "appeared to the public in something like his true character and at something like his full stature."

In my previous book, *Houdini: The Untold Story*, I endeavored to separate the facts from the myths circulated about the great escapologist's career. In this volume, the most intriguing illustrations I could find have been gathered, along with more material on the many-sided mystifier and pertinent comments by Houdini himself.

Onstage Houdini pulled up his sleeves, turned back his shirt cuffs, and permitted challengers to apply the manacles to his wrists in any way they chose. After freeing himself from the irons at the front, he had his hands secured behind his back.

2

Sensational Escapes

Houdini identified challenge manacles with words calculated to emphasize their impregnability: "Maltby Dead Lock Shackles," "Extraordinary Bean Giant Handcuffs," "Regulation Double Lock Tower Leg-irons," "The Bottle Neck." He riveted attention explaining how one handcuff had been used on "The Dortmund Strangler," how another had secured Charles Peace, Britain's most notorious criminal. Since he would be screened from the audience by a curtained cabinet during difficult releases, the escapologist invited volunteers to examine the structure. They confirmed his statement that assistants with keys or tools were not hidden under the curtains or concealed in the top; they verified his claim that aides could not enter through a trapdoor concealed in the floor of the stage.

Tension in the audience rose when Houdini's assistants closed the curtains on the shackled showman. Chief assistant Franz Kukol heightened it. An Austrian with a black moustache and a gold-braided uniform, Kukol held a stopwatch. Every five seconds he called out the time.

In Glasgow, Houdini had ordered "the largest stopwatch in the world" from a clock-making firm; he installed it on one side of the stage. Those in the uppermost gallery rows, he noted, "could see the second hand as it jumped around the dial."

The passage of time was crucial. A man enclosed in an airtight container has only a limited amount of oxygen to breathe; left submerged under water too long, he will drown. Tied to the mouth of a charged cannon, he must escape before the burning fuse reaches the gunpowder.

Houdini received the cannon challenge from four petty officers stationed at the naval barracks in Chatham, England. Thousands of handbills, heralding the event at Barnard's Palace Theatre, carried ominous words: Unless Houdini was able to free himself in twenty minutes, he would be "blown to Kingdom Come."

The Chatham chief of police visualized a catastrophe: a man blasted to bits before the eyes of men, women, and children. He issued an ultimatum; the cannon could be loaded—but the fuse must not be lit.

Even shorn of the danger factor, a capacity crowd witnessed a performance few would forget. The seamen lashed Houdini to the muzzle of their "8-cwt. Steel Gun," thrusting a rifle between his back and arms, then pulling his hands forward until they could bind his wrists over his chest. A longer rope tethered his upright body to the cannon. They wound and tied his torso and legs, and fastened the rope to an iron ring nailed to the stage.

At the starting signal, Houdini looked down, directing the spotlight and the eyes of the spectators to his feet. Gradually he inched the shoe from one foot and kicked it aside. The second shoe followed. Using his agile toes like fingers, he untied the knots on the ring. This done, he squirmed and twisted to loosen his hands. The police chief needn't have worried; Houdini released himself three minutes before a lighted fuse could have exploded the charge.

Houdini played the role of Jonah in Boston. A "sea monster" had been washed ashore on a Massachusetts beach; the lieutenant governor and several friends challenged the headliner to escape from the interior of what the newspapers identified as a whale-octopus. Houdini accepted the dare. The whale-octopus was trucked to a taxidermist; he slit open one side, hollowed out the interior, sloshed a preservative fluid around in the cavity.

On the stage of Keith's Theater, Houdini clad in a bathing suit, shackled hand and foot, was forced through the slit into the carcass. The opening was then laced together with a heavy chain and padlocked. Larger chains crisscrossed the exterior; assistants covered the carcass with a canopy. It took Houdini fifteen minutes to free himself and emerge. He admitted afterward that the fumes of the taxidermist's arsenic solution had almost overcome him; he said that he had practically had to kick his way out.

In Chicago, challengers sealed Houdini like a letter in a man-sized

The Jail-Breaker... Harry Houdini Dec 12 — 1902

I don't look very dangerous

To my friend Goldstone
merry X mas

Houdini's Christmas greeting to Will Goldston in 1902 misspelled Will's name. Harry once spelled a name three different ways in a single hastily written note.

envelope. In Salt Lake City, he stretched out in a coffin; the top was fastened down and the coffin enclosed in a burial vault. Los Angeles postmen padlocked him in a government mail pouch. The University of Pennsylvania varsity team chain-laced him inside a mammoth football. In other cities, furnituremakers secured him inside a rolltop desk, and a submarine crew bolted him inside a diving suit. After each escape, no trace of any tear or break, indicating the point of his exit, could be found.

These feats, it should be stressed, were extra added attractions. His regular act featured challenge shackle releases and Metamorphosis, his trunk illusion. So many imitators in Europe and America copied this routine that he discarded it in 1908 and released himself from a straitjacket in full view and from a covered, padlocked, water-filled iron can. Then, in 1912, at the Circus Busch in Berlin, he introduced his greatest stage creation, the Water Torture Cell.

Houdini enthused in a letter from Germany to his friend Will Goldston

While Houdini wore his coat for preliminary stage releases, he stripped it off and tossed it aside for more dramatic feats.

in London that the new escape was "without doubt the greatest spectacular thing ever witnessed on the stage." For fifteen years it was to baffle and thrill audiences on both sides of the Atlantic.

Other mystifiers crammed as many as fifty feats into a vaudeville turn; Houdini offered two. For the first five minutes of the twenty-minute presentation, he carefully explained every detail of the formidable Water Torture Cell. Less than six feet high, less than three feet square, the tank was made of watertight, metal-lined, solid mahogany. At the front, an inch-thick plate-glass window gave an unobstructed view of the interior. The top consisted of a pair of hinged mahogany stocks. Once his feet were enclosed, they could not be withdrawn through the small ankle holes. The stocks, Houdini said, would be latched; a solid steel frame would be fitted snugly around them; then the frame would be locked to the upper part of the tank. To make his release yet more difficult, after the tank had been filled with water, a steel grille, considerably smaller than the interior of the tank, would be lowered inside it.

It was absolutely impossible, Houdini emphasized, for the submerged prisoner to get into a position where he could reach the stocks with his hands. In addition to the top being locked, the tank was secured by steel bands. Houdini offered a thousand dollars to anyone who could prove he received air while immersed in the water.

Before attempting this, the most mystifying stage release of his career, Houdini announced he would perform the East Indian Needle Feat. He invited a dozen spectators to the stage. While they examined two packages of

needles and a spool of thread, he stripped off his coat, then rolled up his sleeves. Asking the volunteers to verify that his mouth was empty, he opened it wide.

Extending his tongue for the needles, he swallowed them, then, a few moments later gulped down a length of thread. Taking a swallow of water "to wash them down," he again opened his mouth for another inspection.

Reaching between his lips, he pulled out six inches of thread. An assistant held the end as Houdini slowly backed away, his side to the audience. Out came the needles, glittering in the spotlight, threaded, evenly spaced, along the strand.

Acknowledging the applause, Houdini said he would now leave the stage to change his clothes for the Water Torture Cell. Music played as volunteers from the audience probed the tank; then Houdini's assistants, dipping brass pails into a cauldron, filled it to the brim. On the floor under the tank, and extending several feet in each direction, was a piece of canvas. The sides were fastened to a larger wooden frame on the floor. This protected the stage from the splashing water.

Returning in a blue swimsuit, Houdini rested prone on a mat as the heavy mahogany stocks were snapped shut around his ankles. He raised his head and torso so the steel frame could pass over his body and be fitted securely to the stocks. After the grille had been inserted in the center of the tank, ropes attached to the frame hauled him aloft.

Hanging head downward, Houdini signaled to be lowered. Members of the audience watched his entry into the water through the glass front of the

CARDIFF
EMPIRE

QUEEN STREET

PROPRIETORS · · · · · · · · · · MOSS EMPIRES, LIMITED.
Managing Director · · · · · · · · · · Mr. FRANK ALLEN.
Acting Manager · · · · · · · · · · HERBERT J. TAYLOR.

MONDAY, JAN. 6th, 1913 and TWICE NIGHTLY
AT 6.45 AND 9.0 DURING THE WEEK.

THE WORLD-FAMOUS SELF-LIBERATOR!

HOUDINI

Presenting the Greatest Performance of his Strenuous Career, liberating himself after being Locked in a

WATER TORTURE
CELL

Houdini's own Invention, whilst Standing on his Head, his Ankles Clamped and Locked above in the Centre of the Massive Cover. A Feat which borders on to the Supernatural.

£200 Houdini offers this sum to anyone proving that it is possible to obtain air in the upside-down position in which he releases himself from this WATER-FILLED TORTURE CELL.

CASELLI SISTERS
Vocalists and Dancers

HAPPY TOM
PARKER
COMEDIAN AND DANCER

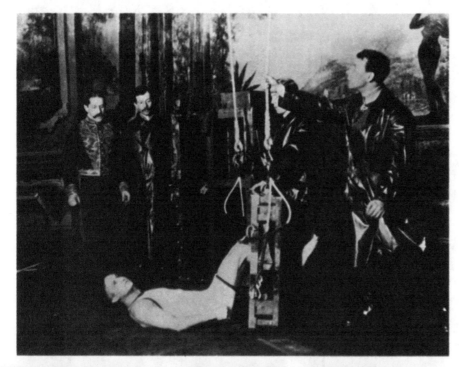

Franz Kukol (top left) supervised the staging of the Water Torture Cell escape. As soon as Houdini had been lowered into the water, the cabinet was pushed forward, then closed to mask his method of release.

Houdini's daring jump into the Charles River from
Harvard Bridge attracted thousands of spectators
from Boston and Cambridge in 1908.

In December of the following year, he leapt
from the upper deck of a tugboat into Liverpool's
Mersey River.

Waiting assistants in a rowboat were ready to dive
to assist him if an emergency developed or to help
him aboard when he swam alongside.

tank. Assistants rapidly unhitched the ropes, locked the frame to the tank, fastened the outer steel bands, then moved a cabinet forward to shroud the tank from view.

An assistant, gripping an axe, stood by the cabinet, ready to rush in and smash the glass should Houdini fail to escape in the allotted time. The orchestra emphasized the danger of his drowning by playing "Asleep in the Deep." As the two-minute mark approached, the frowning assistant peeked through the curtains and raised his axe. Suddenly, Houdini yanked the curtains aside and, dripping wet, stepped forward. He smiled, extended his arms, and bowed. A torrent of applause broke the tension.

Unlike other headliners in the vaudeville era, Houdini worked as hard devising and presenting newsmaking publicity stunts as he did behind the footlights. First came releases from restraints in police headquarters, then naked jail breaks. These received extensive newspaper coverage, but only a few dozen witnesses at most could see them. His next step was to develop an outdoor feat to attract larger numbers of potential ticket buyers.

He began by escaping, after being handcuffed, from a nailed and roped, iron-banded wooden box submerged in a river; then, during a cross-country American tour in 1906, he made the first of many bridge leaps.

An exciting but untrue legend about one of these leaps is dramatized in the Houdini biography written by Harold Kellock. Bess, the magician's wife, recalled for him her anguish at hearing Detroit newsboys shouting in the streets, "Houdini dead! Houdini drowned in river!" She immediately sent for the papers. A few moments after they arrived, Houdini himself entered the hotel room: "His head was still dripping, and he was blue with cold, but he was alive." He told her a hole had been cut in the frozen river for his leap from the Belle Island Bridge. Underwater he had released his shackled hands, but the strong current of the Detroit River swept him away from the opening. He could not find it when he came up beneath the ice. He filled his lungs from the air in the small space between the ice and the water, then much later saw the end of a rope being lowered into the river. He swam toward it.

Houdini liked to tell this under-ice story; and he frequently elaborated on it. He said he swam in ever-widening circles to reach the opening in the ice; the same circling technique, he added, that the captain of an ocean liner uses in rescuing a passenger who has fallen overboard. Usually Houdini singled out Detroit as the place where the harrowing episode occurred, but he sometimes named Pittsburgh and Bremen as the scene of the near disaster. He did make a—for him—routine jump from the Belle Island Bridge in Detroit on November 27, 1906 (not on December 2, as indicated in Houdini

Houdini's jumps from
bridges were seen by
onlookers in boats.

Other spectators on
the shore watched his
feat from a distance.

In Brighton, England, Houdini drew a crowd though there was a heavy rain the day he dove from a high ladder.

In Paris, he leapt from the wall of the Morgue into the Seine, though officials had denied him permission for a jump.

In Birmingham, England, on December 15, 1908, he plunged into the Edgbaston Reservoir and escaped underwater.

A *Mahatma* ad in 1899 reveals that even then Houdini knew how to sell himself to agents.

souvenir books); though the day was cold, the river was not frozen. His wife repeated the fabrication in the Kellock biography after her husband's death, and so it entered the popular mythology about Houdini.

Perhaps the story was initially suggested by a front-page headline in the *Philadelphia North American* on May 15, 1908: HOUDINI SHACKLED, LEAPS INTO RIVER, ALMOST DROWNED. Ten thousand spectators had watched him jump from the Market Street Bridge; a long minute and nine seconds passed before his head emerged above the water.

Earlier that May, more thousands had gathered for his noontime leap from Harvard Bridge into the Charles River, which divides Boston from Cambridge. The mayors of both cities looked on as Houdini, standing on the platform erected for the occasion, removed the overcoat covering his swimsuit and flexed his arms. Patrolman John Griffiths handcuffed Houdini's wrists behind his back, applied shackles to his arms, and connected the latter with a chain that circled his neck.

Houdini climbed to the top of the bridge railing, poised as a stiff breeze

Sensational Escapes

40

rumpled his hair, then jumped feetfirst into the Charles River. Women shrieked as he vanished beneath the water. Small boats stationed under the bridge and to the sides headed for the point of splashdown. Five, ten, fifteen, twenty, twenty-five, thirty seconds passed. Still no sign from below. At the thirty-five–second mark, Houdini bobbed up, about six feet from the point where he had entered the water. He held the chains and cuffs in one hand, brandishing them toward the sea of faces peering from the bridge. One man expressed the feeling of the entire crowd, *The Boston American* reported. "He did it—darned if he didn't," he exclaimed over and over.

In cities without a convenient river, Houdini would jump from the highest available structure into some smaller body of water. On October 13, 1907, in Denver, after Chief Detective Willis Loomis had manacled him on the roof of the City Park band pavilion, he leapt into the lake.

He also jumped from the top of the wall surrounding the Paris morgue into the Seine; dove headfirst from Queen's Bridge, Melbourne, into the Yarra; plunged into the Spree from the Frederichstrasse Bridge in Berlin. Still seeking a sensational open-air feat that could be watched by immense crowds and performed in cities not on waterways, he perfected the upside-down straitjacket release. From Connecticut to California, it proved its worth.

Fifty thousand people, jammed shoulder to shoulder, front to back, stood in the streets of downtown Baltimore on April 26, 1916, to see the greatest free show in town. Rigged to the top of the Sunpapers Building on the southeast corner of Baltimore and Charles streets, was a block and tackle, with a large iron hook at its lower end, extending down to a platform on the pavement. Houdini removed his hat, his overcoat and jacket, then thrust his arms into the sleeves of a five-strap straitjacket held by two uniformed policemen. They tugged the canvas-and-leather restraint together behind his back, buckled the three leather straps. Houdini folded his sheathed arms across his chest. The officers strained until the thongs on the closed ends of the sleeves were also firmly fastened at the back.

Houdini dropped to a sitting position on the platform; his assistants, James Collins and James Vickery, wrapped padding around his ankles and lashed them to the hook of the block and tackle.

Slowly Houdini was hauled fifty feet in the air, head downward. Franz Kukol took out his stopwatch. He shouted, "Go!" The struggle the crowd had assembled to see began.

Houdini twisted, contorted, and thrashed in the air like a frenzied barracuda trying to break a fisherman's line. In a minute and a half, his face getting redder by the second as blood rushed to his head, he had forced his right arm over his head; and his deft fingers, pressing through the canvas,

Upside-down straitjacket release in Toronto, Canada, on the afternoon of October 18, 1916, to raise money for the British Red Cross Fund.

Throngs blocked traffic in cities across
the nation when Houdini hung by his
ankles high above downtown streets.

Strapped in securely, he soon began twisting
and turning in the canvas and leather
restraint, trying to undo a strap at the back.

released the thong from its stay. Spectators cheered, not only those in the streets, but also office workers who threw open their windows and leaned out for a closer view of the spectacle.

At the one-minute-and-fifty-seconds mark, Houdini had wrenched his left arm free. In another minute, he had the wide strap extending from front to back between his legs undone. Then he started the tortuous process of edging the jacket down bit by bit until he could pull it over his head. Thirty seconds later, the straitjacket dropped to the street. The crowd went wild; even the policemen on the platform applauded. Still dangling at the end of the rope, Houdini smiled, extended his arms in acknowledgment, and bending from the waist, took a bow upside down in the air.

The Baltimore *Sun* said this escape brought downtown traffic to a standstill and attracted the largest street mob since the Great Baltimore Fire of 1904. As a boy, I met a secretary who confessed she owed a debt to Houdini. She had worked in the building on the northwest corner of Baltimore and Charles streets. While her superiors were gaping from their windows, she walked across the hall and successfully applied for a job with much higher pay.

Only once did an outdoor release fail to attract business to a theatre where Houdini performed. After his tremendous success in Europe in 1900 produced a great demand for handcuff acts, Houdini brought his brother, Theo, to Germany. Billed as Hardeen, Theo became Harry's principal competitor. Taller and heftier than Houdini, Hardeen, a fine performer, also gained fame. He, too, met manacle challenges, leapt from bridges, and utilizing information Harry had given him, released himself from jails.

The brothers were booked at rival theatres in Oakland, California, in November 1915. As a prank, Hardeen hired small boys to distribute thousands of printed cards bearing his picture, his name, and the name of the Pantages Theatre where he was playing to the thousands who had come to see Houdini squirm suspended in the restraint. The crowd, thinking the man in the air was appearing at the Pantages Theatre, flocked there, and not to the Orpheum.

Houdini had a sense of humor; he enjoyed a good joke; but when volunteers from the audience tried to be funny as they bound him, he squelched their attempts at levity. Suspense was an important ingredient of his act; laughter broke the mood.

Lonney Haskell, a popular vaudeville comedian, introduced Houdini when he appeared for a charity benefit at the Polo Grounds in New York. Haskell stayed on the platform while policemen strapped Houdini in a straitjacket. Haskell drew attention away from the action, saying Houdini wasn't so marvelous—he couldn't get out of a Times Square traffic snarl. The audience laughed; Houdini scowled. Suddenly to his surprise Haskell felt a swift kick in the shins and heard a sharp command to be quiet and get off the stage. Houdini, still bound, had rolled across the platform to deliver the message. Afterward he apologized, explaining that jokes were fine at the end of his act but not during it.

Houdini enjoyed it as much as the audience the night a male member of a vaudeville team heard a very loud noise banging backstage in the theatre and ad-libbed, "That's Houdini, he forgot his key and is trying to get into his dressing room." The magician didn't object then or later when, during subsequent performances, the comedian arranged for stagehands to make a similar ear-splitting racket so he could use the line as part of his regular routine.

The police estimated one hundred thousand Washingtonians saw Houdini wriggle free from a suspended straitjacket, rigged to the Munsey Building in April 1916. The *Washington Times* reported that this was "the biggest crowd ever assembled in Washington at one place except for the inauguration of a President." Woodrow Wilson had occupied the presidential box at Keith's Theatre the year before. He had complimented Houdini after the show: "I envy your ability to escape from tight places. Sometimes I wish I were able to do the same." The day Houdini drew the enormous crowd in the nation's capital, President Wilson was speaking before a joint session of Congress, warning the German government that further submarine raids upon unarmed American merchant ships would force reprisals. Pictures of Houdini's escape were crowded off the front page of the *Washington Times* by the story headlined BREACH WITH GERMANY OVER U-BOATS IMMINENT.

Though the lawmakers were embroiled in discussion, they welcomed diversion. The appearance of the Keith star in the Senate's Visitors' Gallery that Saturday afternoon created a stir. The presiding officer, Vice-President Thomas Marshall, looked up and waved at Houdini. Soon a page delivered a note, inviting him to Marshall's chamber. A recess was called; Houdini, always ready to entertain at a moment's notice, mystified the senators with card magic.

While Houdini was able to cajole police in Los Angeles, San Francisco, Pittsburgh, Chicago, and other large cities to allow him to disrupt downtown traffic, New York City officials steadfastly refused to issue a permit for him to dangle over Broadway. Late in 1917, Houdini as president of the Society of American Magicians joined with the Junior Patriots of America to stage a gala benefit at the New York Hippodrome for the bereaved families

Once he had forced an arm over his head, he could work with his fingers through the canvas and start pulling the jacket down.

With both sleeves unstrapped at the rear, by sheer muscle power he inched the jacket off and away.

Extending his arms as the crowd cheered, Houdini took a bow upside down in the air. This produced tumultuous applause.

Three attractions in the nation's capital: Houdini, then appearing
at Keith's Theatre, suspended in the air to the left; the Treasury
Building to the right; and the monument to the first President of
the United States in the distance.

Note the safety line attached to Houdini's left ankle. If by some unforeseen accident the heavier suspending rope failed, the safety line would prevent his crashing head first in the street.

A wooden beam extending from an open window supports the block-and-tackle lifting device in this instance. The safety line is held by one of Houdini's aides braced near a window three floors below.

CHALLENGE!

I, G. W. HOUGHTON, Champion All-round Swimmer of Great Britain, do hereby CHALLENGE "HOUDINI," of the Pavilion Music Hall, Liverpool, to ESCAPE FROM

A LARGE IRON CHEST

constructed on the style of a safe, after it is filled to the top with water. To prove to the Public that I am not asking him to perform an impossible feat, I will undertake **to escape from this Iron Chest after it is filled with water** in less than six (6) minutes, and defy "HOUDINI" to duplicate the performance.

G. W. HOUGHTON,

Champion Scientific Swimmer of the World and Holder of World's Records for several aquatic feats.

9 WALKER ST., WEST DERBY RD.   L'POOL, JAN. 12th, 1909.

The above Challenge is accepted by HOUDINI ; contest to take place 2nd House, Friday night, Jan. 15th, 1909, on stage of Pavilion, Lodge Lane, L'pool.

The Iron Chest is now on view in front of the Pavilion Music Hall.

Liverpool challenge—to get free from an iron chest "filled to the top with water."

Chatham dare—to escape after being tied to the muzzle of a gun with a 20-minute fuse.

A CHALLENGE FROM THE
NAVAL BARRACKS.

MR. HARRY HOUDINI.   CHATHAM, February 14th, 1911.
Dear Sir,—

We CHALLENGE you to stand in front of a loaded Government 8-cwt. Steel Gun, to which we will secure you, insert a fuse which will burn 20 minutes, and if you fail to release yourself within that time you will be blown to Kingdom Come.

In lashing you to the muzzle of the gun, we will place a rifle barrel between your arms behind your back, bringing your hands on your breast, where we will securely lash them. Your feet we will tie off to an iron ring which we will nail into the floor. Your body we will lash against the muzzle of the gun in such a manner that we believe it will be impossible for you to free yourself.

Test must take place in full view of the Public.

Awaiting your reply, we beg to remain.

Petty Officer J. PHILPOTT.   Petty Officer B. H. JARVIS.
Petty Officer H. S. SMAILES.   Petty Officer W. MUDDOCK.

THE ABOVE CHALLENGE HAS BEEN ACCEPTED
For SECOND PERFORMANCE, FRIDAY, Feb. 17th, at BARNARD'S PALACE THEATRE, CHATHAM.

GARLAY & CO., LTD., CHATHAM

of the men who had perished on the torpedoed transport ship *Antilles*. Elsa Maxwell, an energetic young woman who later became America's most publicized party-giver, convinced the mayor to override the police commissioner's objections. Houdini duly hung by his heels near Times Square as magicians passed out handbills heralding the charity show and their wives sold thrift stamps and war bonds in the street.

The open-air straitjacket escapes were far less dangerous than the manacled leaps into water from a bridge or the escapes from a submerged crate. Even so, a safety rope was moored to Houdini's ankles to prevent him from being battered against the facade of a building by a strong wind and to stop him from crashing headfirst on the pavement should the lifting device fail.

"Human beings don't like to see other human beings die," Houdini said, "but they do love to be on the spot when it happens."

Gashes inflicted on his wrists during challenge handcuff releases and the bruises suffered on his ankles, despite protective padding, during upside-down escape feats healed. Other injuries were more troublesome. Houdini once underestimated the depth of an indoor pool into which he dived; the resulting scar on his head served to remind him to be more precise in the future. At least five times he broke bones in his wrists or ankles. In Detroit, an overzealous challenger fastened the leather straps so tightly around a bag containing Houdini that the pressure broke a blood vessel in his kidney. He hemorrhaged several days before the bleeding stopped. After that, he always slept with a pillow under his side to ease the pain.

Only the quick action of Franz Kukol, his chief assistant, saved Houdini from a bizarre death by drowning. In England, he had accepted a challenge to escape from a padlocked can of beer. Anxious because of the long delay, Kukol entered the cabinet and found Houdini, a teetotaler, overcome by the alcohol, which had seeped through the pores of his body.

Houdini's rivals had their woes, too. Dick Gauss, a Massachusetts escapologist, had been booked as the opening-day attraction at Canobie Lake Park with a submerged-box escape. On a raft far from shore, the manacled Gauss, while stepping into the wooden crate, slipped on the wet planking and overturned the raft. Gauss could not swim; he floundered until a friend rescued him.

At least three men lost their lives attempting manacled dives: one, Richardo, jumped from a bridge in Bavaria and never surfaced.

Harry Orlando, who plunged into the Ohio River from a trestle, was more fortunate. Swimmers among the crowd saw him land flat on the water. They dived in and pulled him ashore. Several of Orlando's ribs had been broken, and there were other internal injuries.

Weighted down with handcuffs, chains, and
an iron ball, Houdini freed himself
beneath the surface of a San Francisco pool.

Leg-ironed, manacled, and chained to a
ladder, with his neck enclosed in a steel collar
by challengers from the audience, Houdini
escaped in 12 minutes.

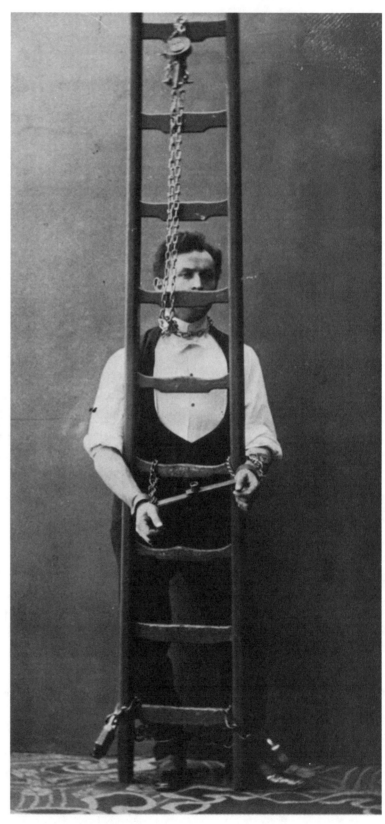

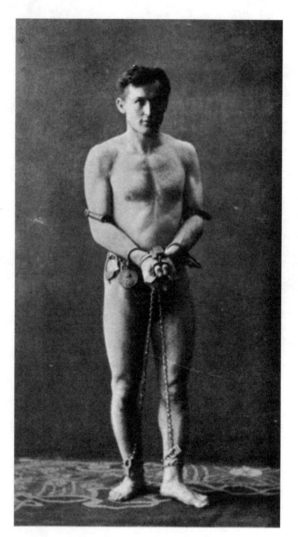

Though he wore a loincloth when these photographs were taken in Germany, Houdini always submitted to a thorough examination before making an escape from prison.

HARRY HOUDINI THE JAIL BREAKER

INTRODUCING HIS LATEST & GREATEST

PRISON CELL & BARREL MYSTERY

HOUDINI is strapped & locked in a barrel placed in a police cell which is also locked and in less than 2 seconds changes places. £100. WILL BE PAID TO ANYONE FINDING TRAPS, PANELS OR FALSE DOORS IN THE CELL.

A variation of Houdini's substitution trunk illusion. Strapped inside a barrel, locked inside a "cell," he released himself. An assistant was then found where Houdini had been.

Hardeen presenting another unusual Houdini creation—an escape from a padlocked water can after the can had been enclosed and locked in a thoroughly examined wooden container.

David Brashur, a nine-year-old boy in Philadelphia, told his playmates he could get out of an old packing case "just like Houdini." As his friends gleefully finished hammering in the nails, they heard a muffled wail. The youngsters smashed open the box; the groaning boy had a four-inch splinter in his abdomen.

Twenty minutes after Maurice Raymond had been shackled, then nailed inside a challenge crate in Rochester, Pennsylvania, distraught aides rushed inside the cabinet, pried off the lid, and found Raymond unconscious. He was hurried to a hospital. Doctors there said a few more minutes in the air-tight container would have killed him.

Houdini clipped these items from newspapers and pasted them in scrapbooks. He was distressed to read, during a tour to the West Coast in 1923, that a seventeen-year-old youth had strangled himself, while hanging by the neck from a rope in a Vancouver cellar attempting to duplicate one of the great escapologist's most dangerous feats. Two later accounts scotched this rumor; police investigators said a suicide note had been found near Harry Porter's dangling body.

"When Magic Didn't Work," an article in the April 18, 1925, issue of *Collier's* magazine, told of Houdini's close calls with death. He himself supplied the basic material; the writer distorted the details. Houdini freed himself from padlocked, water-filled cans while handcuffed—not after having been "fettered and strait-jacketed." The news-making escape from the interior of the whale-octopus had been staged at Keith's Theatre in Boston—not at the seaside with the carcass of the beast underwater. Houdini had been shackled to stakes in a San Francisco park, releasing himself after a ring of brushwood had been saturated with gasoline and lighted, but this was not the near-incineration episode the article made it out to be.

The *Collier's* article stated that Houdini had the "narrowest squeak" of his career in Santa Ana, California. The tale is told in gripping terms. Houdini bet that if he were handcuffed and buried alive in sand six feet beneath the sod, he would still be able to escape to the surface. Keeping the sand from being packed too tightly above his body, he braced himself at the bottom of the pit for the struggle. A sudden realization that corpses are interred at this depth gave him "the first thrill of horror" he had ever experienced as a daredevil. Panicking momentarily—violating one of his cardinal principles, to keep control of himself under the most trying conditions—he used up some of the precious oxygen needed to sustain him in his fight for freedom. Forcing his way upward, he felt himself weakening and tried to shout for help. Then the strongest human instinct—survival—overcame his fears, and he made it to the surface.

Houdini had indeed been buried alive in California, but not to win a

Sensational Escapes

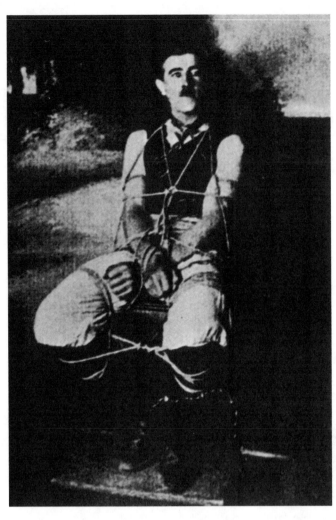

Houdini holds a replica of the *Daily Mirror* handcuffs he escaped from.

A German imitator of the "Elusive American" billed himself as Harry Haudyni. Others who capitalized on Houdini's success took such similar names as Nordini and Mourdini.

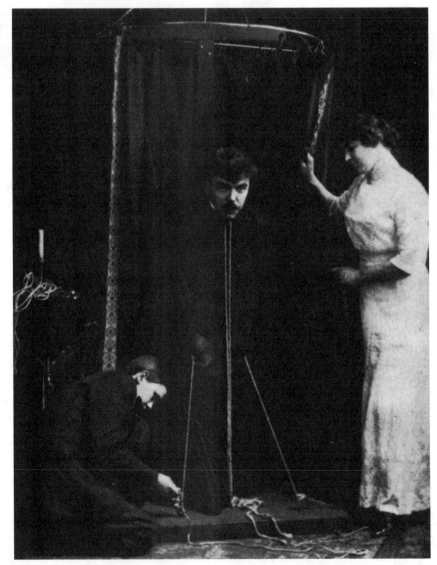

An American magician, performing in California, featured a feat of escapology unlike those Houdini had staged so effectively.

Performers in Europe, Asia, Australia,
and America attempted to duplicate
Houdini's underwater releases.

Empress, one of several women escape artists
who tried to reproduce Houdini's stage act. She
never attempted his naked cell escape.

GRAND THEATRE, CHURCH ST. BLACKPOOL

PROPRIETOR AND MANAGER — MR. T. SERGENSON.
RESPONSIBLE DIRECTOR OF VARIETIES — MR. ALFRED SELWYN.

MONDAY, DECEMBER 6th, 1909, for Six Nights
7-0 — Twice Nightly — 9-0
Doors Open at 6-30 and 8-45.

The One and Only Lady Masterpiece

EMPRESS
THE CLEVER LADY OF MYSTERY.
In her Wonderful and Startling Escapes, including
Escape from Police Handcuffs, Packing Case, and Straight Jacket.
The escape from the Straight Jacket and Packing Case performed in full view of the audience
Also the Greatest Sensation of Modern Times—

☞ THE WATER MYSTERY ☜
Escape from an Iron Tank filled with water and locked with padlocks which may be brought
by any member of the Audience. One of the most daring feats ever attempted by a Lady.
Must be seen to be believed. Something New Every Night.

Owing to his Enormous Success

☞ HARRY MAYNARD
Has been retained for One Week Longer.

Papa Buys Fireworks	A Most Instructive and Interesting Film—
Shows the trouble caused by Father putting a Packet in his Tail Pocket which catches fire, and eventually is put out by the Fire Hose. A Scream from start to finish.	**Sardine Fishing** From start to finish. Mending Nets—The Fleet leaving for the Grounds—Trawling —Packing in Tins ready for the Table.
Another comical Picture is the	A Highly Dramatic Picture—
Never Late Clerk	**Old Kentucky**

Pleasing Engagement of
CARLOTTA MAYSON
A Singer of Sensible Songs.
The Pick of the Picture World is
A NOBLE FORGIVENESS

POPULAR PRICES : Stalls 1/6; Grand Circle 1/-; Upper Circle and Pit 6d. ; Gallery 3d.
Box Office open Daily 10 a.m. to 5-0 p.m. No Extra Charge for Booking. For Seats address
Letters or Telegrams to Box Office, Grand Theatre. Telephone No. 73. Telegraphic Address,
"Grand, Blackpool." No Money Returned. No Tickets Exchanged,
Advertising Inspector, Mr. J. Deakin.

A British magician devised an escape from a small, locked box that encased his torso.

Jean Hugard added a Houdini water can and a straitjacket release to his show when Houdini came to Australia in 1910.

bet. Visualizing a sensational exploitation feat, he conducted an experiment while his assistants stood by, ready to dig down quickly should there be difficulties. There were. His notes said, "I tried out 'Buried Alive' in Hollywood and nearly (?) did it. Very dangerous; the weight of the earth is killing."

Still the idea intrigued him. He devised a method for escaping from a coffin after it had been buried in a large tank with glass sides on the stage. Though he had a poster made to advertise this feat, it did not prove to be as exciting to spectators as he expected.

Two of Houdini's most fantastic escape conceptions were never tried. He imagined himself leaping shackled from the roof of the world's tallest skyscraper—at that time, the Woolworth Building in New York City—and freeing himself as he descended by parachute to the street. He also visualized himself being nailed in a packing crate on the banks of the rapids above Niagara Falls. As thousands watched, the box would be swept over the Falls and disintegrate in the whirlpool below. When everyone believed he had been destroyed, he would mysteriously reappear on the shore.

Houdini had no qualms about blending fiction with fact in his quest for publicity. During his tour of Britain in 1920, he arranged for a series of weekly articles "by Houdini himself" to appear in *Kinema Komics*. These imaginary escapades were so popular that long after he returned to the United States, they continued to appear. Like other stories that appeared in this periodical under the byline of film stars, they were written by British journalists.

Another farfetched series, "Houdini's Schooldays," ran in *Merry and Bright*, a penny-and-a-half comic paper. The fictional school was sited not in Wisconsin, but near "Burnash," an English town. While a pupil at "Rathgar," young Houdini conjured, played the violin, excelled at billiards, and outwitted older bullies.

Later, in 1924, H. P. Lovecraft, a writer whom Houdini had introduced to several editors, prepared fictional stories of the magician's experiences from the notes Houdini provided for *Weird Tales*, an American monthly.

As early as 1919, the master of manacles admitted in a newspaper interview that he was aware superstitious spectators credited him with superhuman powers; after his death, he said they would talk about him even more.

P. T. Barnum achieved lasting fame with ingenious publicity stunts he devised for the stars of his shows, among them, Tom Thumb the midget; Jenny Lind, the Swedish singer; and Jumbo, the elephant. Houdini surpassed the earlier showman, publicizing a single attraction—himself.

Houdini said the world might forget his sensational escape feats,
but it would always remember him as a pioneer aviator.

3

First to Fly over Australia

Along with the many pieces of baggage Houdini invariably carried with him during his travels, two unusually long new crates and several shorter ones were loaded aboard the *Malwa* in Marseilles on the morning of January 7, 1910. Carefully packed in the heavy boxes were the dismantled parts of an airplane. Scarcely more than six years before, at a field near Kitty Hawk, North Carolina, Wilbur and Orville Wright had demonstrated that a heavier-than-air machine could fly. It was a time when pioneering aviators were competing to be the first in the air over a country or continent. With luck, the master magician might make the first successful flight over Australia.

The conquest of the air intrigued Houdini. Several of his predecessors in magic had shared the same fascination. Giovanni Giuseppe Pinetti, the most famous Italian mystifier of the late eighteenth century, had invested heavily in balloon experiments while in Russia. Andrew Oehler, a German-born conjurer, had attracted crowds in New Orleans and Mexico City with similar ascensions. Garnerin, a French showman, had celebrated the coronation of Napoleon by ballooning from Paris to Rome in twenty-four hours. Etienne Gaspard Robertson, a Belgian, staged aerial spectacles throughout Europe.

Late in 1908, Houdini had told a British reporter he planned to take his manacled leaps to new heights. He had offered the owner of a Wright Brothers airplane five thousand dollars to fly him over London's West End. He hoped to parachute down—releasing his hands en route—and land in Piccadilly Circus. A later newspaper account said the daring venture had been postponed; a dependable way of releasing a passenger by parachute had not yet been devised.

While performing at the Hansa Theatre in Hamburg, Germany, in November 1909, Houdini learned that Hans Grade, a German pilot, was to demonstrate his flying skill with a biplane at the local racetrack. Earlier, in Bork, this aviator had flown the first piece of air mail on record. (At this period, of course, most flights were of short duration. More time was taken preparing airplanes for takeoff than was spent in the air.)

Houdini, like the other spectators at the Hamburg racetrack, cheered as the biplane rose from the ground, circled the track, and landed intact. Until then, Houdini had visualized himself parachuting from a plane; now he was seized by the urge to learn how to fly himself. What a publicity coup it would be if he could make the first pioneering flight in Australia during his upcoming tour! If he arrived too late for that, there was still a chance of being the first in the air over South America.

Houdini ran across the field, shouldered his way through the mob surrounding Grade, introduced himself, and fired a volley of questions. Several days later a biplane designed by Alberto Santos-Dumont—a wealthy young Brazilian who had made the first successful flight in Paris in 1901—and built by Voisin Frères arrived in Hamburg. Houdini paid the equivalent of five thousand dollars for the machine; with it came a short, plump French mechanic named Brassac. The magician had hired Brassac to assemble the parts and to instruct him in the mysteries of flight.

Twice nightly on the stage of the Hansa, Houdini released himself from challenge shackles. His mornings were occupied by less strenuous activities in Wandsbek. The commander of the German army troops had given Houdini permission to use the Hufaren parade grounds as an air field; he rented a shed for six hundred and fifty marks to serve as a hangar.

Always uneasy in the driver's seat of an automobile, Houdini relaxed during the practice sessions in the plane. The operating procedure was not complicated. The steering wheel, attached to a rudder, was turned to change

Once he had mastered the controls of his newly acquired Voisin biplane, Houdini was eager to fly.

He made his first successful ascent on November 26, 1909, above a German army parade ground.

The Houdinis; James Vickery; Brassac, the French mechanic; and an unidentified man pose for a picture en route to Melbourne.

The Houdinis went sightseeing when the ship reached Ceylon. He had never performed in this part of the world.

He searched without success for a native magician in the Fiji Islands.

The Houdinis and Brassac ignore the photographer; James Vickery stares into the lens.

Houdini intended to issue an illustrated book about this trip around the world.

Pictures such as this were to have accompanied the text.

the direction of the kitelike machine; the control lever was pushed forward for elevation, pulled back for descent.

The aluminum propeller blades, four feet long, were kept in motion by a British EN 60–80 horsepower motor. The propellers were small in proportion to the size of the plane; it measured 33 feet 6 inches from tip to tip. Balloon sheeting on the top, bottom, and outer sides of the wings inspired Houdini. Why not put a flying advertisement there? He had his name painted in large letters on the sides. Later he added "No. 1." Whether this was intended to indicate that he was at the top of his theatrical profession or was meant to imply that the plane was the first of a prospective fleet, he failed to say.

Stormy winter weather, high winds, and occasional snowfalls kept the Voisin in the shed while Houdini familiarized himself with the controls. He was impatient to fly, especially after his instructor, Brassac, informed him that a Voisin plane had stayed aloft a full twenty-five minutes at Reims.

Finally, one clear, almost windless morning, the plane was rolled from the shed. Houdini climbed in and gripped the steering wheel. Brassac spun the propellers. The engine raced; the mooring line was released; and the Voisin spurted forward, then rose up several feet in the chilly air. No difficult manacled escape had ever produced in Houdini a thrill equal to the one at that moment. His elation abruptly faded as the plane nosed down. He wrote in his diary that night: "I smashed the machine. Broke Propeller all to heil."

The damage was not as extensive as his words suggested. Still, two weeks passed before a new propeller arrived from Paris, and another good day for flying dawned.

Houdini made his first successful flight over the Hufaren parade grounds on November 26, 1909. Fewer than fifty people were present, but photographers recorded the event for posterity. Houdini sent the pictures to the German press and to publications in England, France, Austria, Belgium, Holland, and the United States. His engagement in Hamburg was prolonged through the month of December.

In Marseilles, Houdini personally supervised the loading of his gear on the *Malwa*. Other magicians in the past had arrived in distant ports to find crates smashed and valuable equipment crushed. Worse yet, important small containers were sometimes lost on the dock. Houdini boarded the ship with his wife, his three stage assistants, and Brassac, the French mechanic; his biplane, an extra motor, and a case of spare parts had been stowed in the hold for the long voyage to Australia.

When the *Malwa* stopped at Port Said, Houdini hurried down the

The crates that carried the dismantled parts of Houdini's plane arrived safely without damage.

They were opened at Digger's Rest, a field near Melbourne, and Brassac assembled the machine.

The wreckage of Banks's plane
was heaped up and hauled away.

Two weeks earlier, Ralph
Banks's Wright biplane had
crashed. Banks is the man
with the open jacket.

On the morning of March 16,
1910, Houdini made a
successful flight over Australia.

While performing in Sydney, Houdini flew above the Rosehill Racecourse.

The tent that served as a hangar for Houdini's Voisin is behind the plane.

With magicians Allan Shaw
and Charles J. Carter,
Houdini visited the grave of
William Henry Harrison
Davenport, an American stage
medium, near Sydney.

William T. Fay, who had worked with the
Davenport Brothers, and his wife welcomed
Houdini's questions about the Davenport séances.

James Vickery supervised the storing of the
Voisin at a warehouse in Peckham, England.

gangplank. The first leg of the trip had been rough. He had been seasick two and a half days. Heights did not affect him; swimming underwater was pleasurable. The mere sight of a steamship, however, caused his stomach to churn.

Houdini watched six native magicians perform on the streets of Port Said. They presented the traditional Egyptian legerdemain with three inverted metal cups and three small balls. The balls disappeared and reappeared, then changed into live baby chicks. "When you have seen one, you have seen them all," Houdini reported. He was even more critical in a letter to an old friend in London: "None of them possess great sleight of hand, and with their loose blouses are enabled to take liberties in getting 'loads' that a European magician could never do. . . . The one that came on the ship is a good talker and entertains the Tourists. His feature was 'cutting the turban' and telling the audience that he would show them the Mango tree. His best feat was *lying*."

The ship's smooth passage through the Suez Canal, with land in view, maintained Houdini's equilibrium temporarily. Then high waves in the Red Sea sent him reeling below deck to his cabin. Two days before the vessel reached Ceylon, he recovered, and on the evening of January 20, he gave an hour-and-twenty-minute magic show for the passengers. "I am as good as when I was young!" he enthused in a letter posted in Colombo.

Attired in a white suit and a tropical sun helmet, Houdini hired rickshas for his wife and for himself. One of his assistants took photographs of the Houdinis. Among Houdini's many unfinished projects was an illustrated autobiography. Pictures taken during his travels were to have been included. After losing the first draft of the text, he never found time to complete it.

Aside from the show at sea and the jaunts ashore, the twenty-nine days between Marseilles and Melbourne had been an agonizing experience. Sick more than half the time, Houdini was able to eat in the ship's dining room only fourteen times, and he lost twenty-eight pounds.

It is doubtful whether he would have subjected himself to this ordeal had not Harry Rickards, the leading Australian impresario, signed a most unusual contract with him. This came about, Houdini wrote in a letter dated June 12, 1909, because of "a little trouble" at the Chelsea Music Hall in London.

> It was of such a nature that the house was sold out at early door money, seats sold on the stage, and thousands turned away. I had three challenges in one night, and Mr. Harry Rickards was in the audience, and I am in possession of a contract which means Australia for 12 weeks, and I am to receive the biggest salary he has ever paid to anyone so far, and I RECEIVE FULL SALARY WHILE ON BOARD THE STEAMER. So I get paid 12 weeks for resting and 12 for working. That is the only condition that I would go all that distance.

Houdini approached the customs inspection in Australia with trepidation, though he rarely had difficulties. An encounter at the Russian frontier in 1903 had been an exception. There the guards had made train passengers open personal letters. One man was forced to remove his shoes; foreign-language newspapers were confiscated. To keep the prying Russians from reading the notes he had written explaining handcuff secrets, Houdini had sealed his desk trunk and sent it back to Germany.

An impromptu trick or two usually eased his way through customs, but even Houdini could not divert the attention of the Australian inspectors from the massive crates containing the parts of his 11,400-pound biplane. The owner of a Wright flying machine already in Australia had posted a bond equivalent to $4,000; Houdini managed to get his Voisin into the country with a mere $750 deposit. These bonds were required to insure that the owners did not sell their planes without informing the import tax collectors.

Harry Rickards had no doubt his new attraction would pack the New Opera House in Melbourne; he billed Houdini as "Absolutely the Greatest and most Sensational Act that has ever been engaged by any Manager."

During his stay Houdini dove—manacled—from Queen's Bridge into the Yarra River; later he jumped—shackled—into a pool in Sydney. After having been rolled in sheets, strapped to the iron frame of a hospital bed, and doused with water, he released himself and wriggled free from a challenge straitjacket. He fully justified Rickard's confidence. His dominant interest at the moment, however, was aviation. Brassac uncrated the plane and assembled it on the field at Digger's Rest, twenty miles from Melbourne. No structure being available to house the Voisin, Houdini bought a three-hundred-dollar tent.

He chose Digger's Rest because a sportsman who also hoped to be first to fly over Australia was experimenting there. The proximity of the two planes drew public interest to the contest.

Ralph B. Banks, proprietor of the Melbourne Motor Garage, had imported a plane built by the Wright brothers but had not yet succeeded in getting it off the ground. If Banks resented the intrusion of a competitor, he did not show it. He and his mechanics sympathized with Houdini when the engine of the Voisin failed to function properly. They themselves had experienced similar problems.

One morning in late February both planes were ready. The day was too windy for flying, Brassac asserted. Reluctantly Houdini agreed with him. They watched morosely as Banks's mechanics prepared for a takeoff. The Wright plane rose a few feet from the ground. Wind rocked the fragile craft; Banks was compelled to make a forced landing.

Once the crated sections of the bi-plane were unloaded, Vickery posed with the workmen.

Houdini.
276 WEST 113 STREET NEW YORK CITY U.S.A.

c/o Day's Agency,
          Effingham House,
                    Arundel St.,

          Strand, LONDON., W.C

          May17th, 1913.

Messrs Mulliners',
          Long Acre,
                    LONDON.

Gentlemen,

          Mr. Donald Stevenson, who is the bearer of this letter has full power to deal with the matter of my Aeroplane.

          Please allow him to view the machine, and when he has satisfied himself that the machine and parts as taken by you are in good condition and everything complete, he has power to settle your account and remove the machine.

                    Yours faithfully,

                    Harry Houdini

The letter Houdini wrote authorizing Donald Stevenson to claim the plane.

BILL MATTER.

FOR WEEK.......... .... AT.............................

THE WORLD-FAMOUS____
HOUDINI
THE ORIGINAL
HANDCUFF KING & JAIL BREAKER

The only living being who ever escaped from the SIBERIAN TRANSPORT VAN in Russia, and who has also ESCAPED from the STRONGEST PRISONS in all parts of the World. Introducing his latest invention, that of escaping out of an AIR-TIGHT GALVANISED IRON CAN filled to the brim with water, and LOCKED with SIX PADLOCKS! Houdini's remarkable ability to remain under water a long time is one of the resources which enable him to accomplish this EXTRAORDINARY trick.

Everybody Invited to bring their own Padlocks

HOUDINI PICTORIAL PRINTING.

SIZE.	REMARKS.
24 Sheet.	
18 Sheet.	
12 Sheet.	
6 Sheet.	
2 Sheet.	
D. C.	

ALL ORDERS for above or any Communications, re same should be addressed to my Permanent Address :-

DAY'S AGENCY, Effingham House,
Arundel Street, Strand, London, W.C.

STAGE PLOT
FOR
HOUDINI'S
Death Defying Mystery.

Street Cloth.

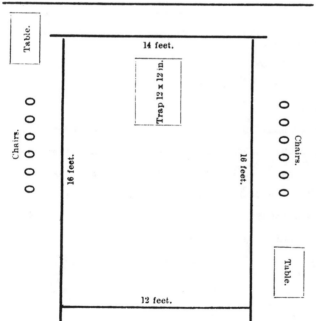

HOUDINI PROPERTY LIST.

Two Large Dressing Rooms, near stage, and Two men dress in any room.

Require about 80 gallons of Water which must be luke-warm, (about 90 Temp. will do).

One Batten 2 x 5 and 14 feet in length.

One Batten 2 x 5 and 12 feet in length.

Two Battens 2 x 5 and 16 feet in length.

Two small Tables (Parlour).

Eighteen bentwood Chairs.

Work in full stage.

Steps from audience to stage to allow committee to come on stage, if possible.

Have a small TRAP made in stage. This Trap must be about 12 x 12 inch, and should be about two feet in the rear of the front cloth drop ; and a large barrel or receptacle must be placed under the stage to catch the 80 gallons of water as it falls through.

The ENTIRE quantity of water is spilled on the stage, and into the receiver underneath the stage. You can secure a HOSE of some description to the end of the TUBE we carry, and this will allow the water to run to any given point you wish.

TARPAULIN that we carry must be hung up to dry after each performance.

DO NOT get anything that is to be Charged to me.

Billing sheet, with stage plot and property list, for the act
featuring Houdini's escape from a padlocked, water-filled can.

He tried again on March first. This time the machine rose twelve feet in the air, abruptly nosedived, then crashed. Though Banks escaped serious injury, his plane was shattered beyond repair. Houdini consoled his rival. Photographs were taken of the wreckage before it was hauled away.

Houdini hurried to the field after his last show each evening; he slept in the tent with the Voisin. Though anxious to get into the air, he had no intention of repeating Banks's mistakes. Two weeks dragged by before the arrival of an ideal day for flying. Shortly after dawn on March 16, 1910, his assistants positioned the Voisin on the planks that served as a runway; a mooring rope extended from a dynamometer to the plane. Brassac checked the controls and the landing gear. A confident Houdini mounted to the seat behind the steering wheel. He adjusted a pair of goggles over his eyes, pulled his cap firmly down on his head, smiled, and waved to his wife. Bess crossed her fingers for good luck.

Brassac spun the propellers. The motor hummed, gained speed, and the plane strained at the mooring line. The indicator hand on the dynamometer advanced until a pull of 340 pounds was reached. Brassac released the mooring rope. The plane shot forward, and up, an unexpected gust of wind tipping it from side to side.

For a moment it seemed the plane would strike a tall gum tree on the edge of the field. Houdini pushed forward on the elevating control; the Voisin skimmed the uppermost branches. The plane circled the field at an estimated fifty miles an hour, then returned to the plank runway for a perfect landing. The first successful flight in Australia had been made—by a man who five months before had taken his first flying lesson.

In his second flight at Digger's Rest Houdini reached an altitude of one hundred feet. Airborne for almost five minutes, he flew approximately seven miles. A Pathé News cameraman recorded another, shorter, two-and-a-half–minute flight; this film was widely distributed to theatre audiences.

Houdini set a new time record—seven minutes and thirty-seven seconds—on March twenty-first. This was attested to by Walter M. Meeks, the official timekeeper, and by an *Argus* reporter with his own stopwatch. Among the sixteen signatures on the eyewitness report was that of his former rival, Ralph Banks.

Australia's number-one airman moved on to Rickards' Tivoli Theatre in Sydney in late March. He doubled on stage and at the Rosehill Racecourse. The press agent for the Tivoli Theatre announced that Houdini would receive $100,000 for ten flights at the track. The magician told a *Daily Telegraph* reporter his Voisin had "flown hundreds of times and had never been

When an imitator performed in Scotland, two of Houdini's assistants were sent to open a show revealing the encroacher's secrets.

Houdini promised to give fifty pounds to the Cottage Hospital in Woolwich, England, if he did not escape from a challenge box.

HOUDINI CHALLENGED

BARNARD'S, WOOLWICH.

THOMAS & EDGE,
Builders and Contractors,
Anglesea Avenue, Woolwich, s.e.
January 3rd, 1905.

Mr. Houdini,

Dear Sir,—Having witnessed ou Trunk Trick, I am inclined to think it is NOT GENUINE, and believe the Box has been specially prepared for the Trick. I should be glad if you would undertake to escape from a Box made of 1-inch Deal, in the form of a Packing Case, securely put together, and the LID NAILED DOWN BY ME, and the Box roped up on the stage.

Yours truly,

H. C. GREENWOOD, Manager.

In accordance with the request contained in the above letter,

HOUDINI

ACCEPTS THE CHALLENGE,

and will allow himself to be

Nailed in the Packing Case

and Roped in Full View of the Audience, on

THURSDAY NIGHT (SECOND HOUSE)

and will attempt to escape therefrom.

If unsuccessful, will forfeit £50 to the Funds of the Cottage Hospital.

(Signed) HARRY HOUDINI.

HOW HANDCUFF TRICKS ARE DONE
BY IMPOSTERS!

Herr Franz Kukol the **CELEBRATED ILLUSIONIST OF VIENNA**, and Mr Geo. Vickery the **MAGICIAN OF LONDON**, beg to inform the general public that they will appear at the large shop No. 23 and 25 NICOLSON STREET, next door to Moss' Empire Music Hall, where they will give performances every half hour, **SHOWING HOW HANDCUFF TRICKS ARE DONE BY ALL IMPOSTERS!**

These gentlemen confess they do not know how HARRY HOUDINI, who is engaged at the GAIETY THEATRE, LEITH, this week, performs his tricks. If they did they would not travel as exposers.

LIKE ALL other BOGUS HANDCUFF IMPOSTERS THEY DO NOT ALLOW ANYONE TO BRING HANDCUFFS.

NO ONE is ALLOWED ON THE STAGE. No one is allowed to examine the trunk they make use of, as **THEY HAVE A TRAP IN THE TOP OF BOX**, similar to other Imitators, and tear open the bottom of the bag they use!

They cannot open any Handcuff unless their own, and they must have a key to fit, just the same as all other Exposers.

THE WHOLE SWINDLE SHOWN FOR A PENNY.

NEXT DOOR TO THE EMPIRE THEATRE
Open from 11 a.m. to 9 p.m.

Facing page: He released himself after being rolled in wet sheets and tied to a hospital bed in several English cities and then in Sydney.

Strapped in a sail-cloth seabag, Houdini rolled and tossed on the stage until with great effort he worked his way out.

The "tank" referred to in this challenge was the iron can that was usually filled with water. Similar dares were also accepted.

CHALLENGE !

MR. HARRY HOUDINI.

Dear Sir—If you will allow the undersigned Trained Nurses and Asylum Warders to roll you in soaking wet sheets, fasten you down with wet linen bandages, and pour several buckets of water over your form after we have secured you down to a hospital bed, we will guarantee that you will not be able to affect your escape.

We warn you that the water will cause the sheets and bandages to shrink and hold you in an absolute helpless condition, from which you will only be too pleased to have us release you.

If this challenge is accepted, kindly let us know a day ahead, so we can make arrangements to have the night off from our Institutions.

If you do not care to make the attempt to escape in full view of the audience, we do not care to go any further with the challenge.

WALTER LITTLE,
21, South Street, Hulme (Royal Infirmary, Manchester, and Monsall Fever Hospital, Newton, Manchester; also of Tuebrook Asylum, Liverpool).

THOS. BATES,
19, Albert Grove, Albert Street, Withington (Chorlton Union Workhouse Lunatic Ward, Manchester, and St. Pancras Workhouse, London).

W. CAHILL,
53, Vernon Street, Moston (Prestwich Asylum).

Houdini accepts the above challenge, and will make the attempt on

Wednesday Evening, Feb. 24th,

AT

Empire, Ashton-under-Lyne,
SECOND HOUSE.

Broadhead & Son, Printers, 25, 11b Street, Manchester.

CHALLENGE !!

Houdini—Dear Sir:

We hereby challenge you to allow four of our employees to fill that tank with our Knickerbocker Beer, and if you accept our defi, name your time, our men will be at your disposal with the required amount of beverage.

Awaiting the favor of an early reply, we remain, very truly yours,

JACOB RUPPERT, Brewers,

3rd AVE. and 90th ST., New York City.

Mr. Jacob Ruppert—Dear Sir:

I hereby accept your challenge to be locked into the tank filled with your beer in which I shall be completely submerged. Kindly send about 80 to 100 gallons. I hereby give you in writing as requested, that, in case of any accident to myself during test no responsibility shall rest upon yourself or any of your employees.

Respectfully yours,

HARRY HOUDINI

This remarkable test will take place at

Hammerstein's VICTORIA THEATRE
42d Street and Broadway, New York City

Tuesday Eve., JAN. 30, 1912

THE LIVERPOOL TARPAULIN MAKERS CHALLENGE HOUDINI

LIVERPOOL, November 23rd, 1910.

Mr. HARRY HOUDINI.

Dear Sir,

We defy you to escape from a restraint that we will manufacture, used in the days of the Sailing Vessels to *restrain the MAD-WITH-GROG Sailors or Desperate Criminals* on the High Seas. We refer to the greatly dreaded *SEABAG*, which has been *abolished on account of the extreme torture* to the Prisoner.

This we intend making from Strong Sail Cloth that has been treated with oil and tar to prevent slipping, and will envelope you from the neck down to and including your feet; on the outside of this you will be encircled with stout heavy canvas straps held into place with adjustable leather straps and steel buckles.

If you accept this challenge we demand at least one day to manufacture the Seabag, and you must make the attempt to *release yourself in full view of the audience.* No cabinets, screens or scenery allowed.

Awaiting your early reply,
We remain,
Yours truly,

J. COVENTRY, 9 Dyson Street, Walton, Liverpool;
J. DANIEL, Elphin Grove, Walton, Liverpool;
J. ED. JONES, 46 Paley Street, Everton, Liverpool.
EMPLOYEES OF ANDREW HOWARD, Manufacturer Tarpaulins, Sail Cloths, Etc., 35 Red Cross Street, Liverpool.

HOUDINI accepts the above Challenge for the Second Performance at the Liverpool Olympia

On Friday Night, Nov. 25th, 1910,
under the condition that the straps or fastenings encircling his neck must not be drawn so that there is any danger of strangulation.

broken." This statement, like the sum the press agent mentioned, was an exaggeration. The interview appeared on April twentieth. Two days later the plane, buffeted by a crosswind, came down with a thud; a landing wheel struck a jagged surface and snapped.

After his second show at the Tivoli on Friday, April 29, Houdini attended a meeting at Sydney Town Hall, where his flight films were shown. He was greeted with cheers and presented with a trophy. Engraved on a plate above a metal bas-relief of the globe showing the continent of Australia flanked by two wings, were the words, "The Aerial League of Australia to H. Houdini for the First Aerial Flight in Australia, March 16, 1910."

Following this gala celebration, Houdini wrote Thomas Driver, a magician in Wellington, New Zealand, "Even if history forgets Houdini, the Handcuff King, it must write my name as the first man to fly here. Not that it will put any jam on my bread."

There were two seats in his plane, but Houdini always flew alone. He lamented to Driver that the Voisin could carry so little fuel; otherwise, he joked, he and his wife would cross the Pacific by air, rather than face another torturous journey by sea.

Houdini completed the last lap of his "voyage around the universe" aboard the *Manuka*—a 4,500-ton vessel of the Canadian Pacific Line— described in his letter to Driver as a "miserable, wretched steamer." After the *Manuka* anchored off Suva in the Fiji Islands, dark-skinned young men rowed out in small boats and dived for silver coins the passengers tossed overboard, surfacing with the coins between their teeth.

Houdini said the swimmers caught the coins underwater with their hands, then put them in their mouths. Another passenger doubted this statement. Houdini offered to prove it. He made a bet that if the best diver's hands were fastened behind his back, the feat would fail. The bet was accepted. Houdini dashed to his cabin, changed to a swimsuit, and returned to the deck with a rope and a pair of handcuffs. The Fiji islander who agreed to make the test rejected the shackles, explaining through an interpreter that they were "too heavy." The islander's wrists were bound with the rope; Houdini's were manacled. They poised to dive. Two coins were thrown over the side; the swimmers splashed down almost simultaneously.

Within a minute, the Fijian's head appeared. Fifteen seconds later, Houdini surfaced; he opened his mouth to display both pieces of silver. He gave the coins to the diver, then collected his winnings from the skeptical passenger.

This was one trick Houdini had no hesitation about explaining. He said it was easy to follow the coins as they dropped through the clear water; the silver reflected the hot rays of the sun. Once below the surface, the es-

Handcuffed, leg-ironed, and chained, Houdini entered a sturdy
packing crate and was nailed inside as reporters and photographers
from New York newspapers observed the procedure.

Collins, the magician's assistant, made sure that
the weights at the sides of the box were secure,
then signaled for it to be lowered beneath the
surface of the East River.

Onlookers in nearby boats watched as the crate
entered the water and, with Collins' aid, began
to sink without tilting.

Each second that passed after the crate had disappeared from view heightened the tension. Would Houdini drown—or escape?

Suddenly Houdini bobbed up far away from the point where the crate had last been seen. He waved and swam to the side of the tug.

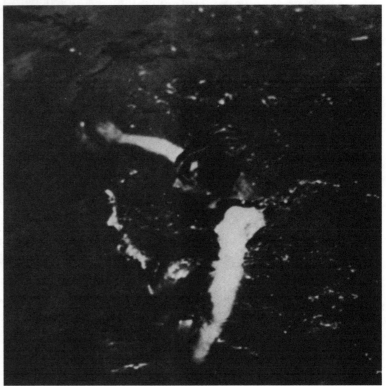

When block and tackles were impractical, the heavy boxes were lowered into rivers by a "seesaw" plank.

capologist released one hand in time to catch both coins. He put them in his mouth, replaced his free hand in the open manacle, then snapped it shut. Characteristically, Houdini claimed he had to move quickly to evade "the man-eating sharks."

Following his aerial triumph in Australia, Houdini lost interest in flying a plane himself but not in aviation. New records for distance and altitude were being established somewhere in the world almost every week. Venturesome pilots gambled with their lives, trying to outdo their competitors. Thirty-five men were killed in crashes in the three-year period ending in 1910; in 1911, the total rose to seventy-six fatalities.

No spectator at the International Air Meet in Chicago in 1911 enjoyed the show more than Houdini. He wrote to his wife, then ill in New York, "At one time I saw twelve planes in the air. I never before saw such wonderful sights." He marveled when four Wright planes took off at three fifteen in the afternoon and stayed aloft until twilight. "Twice," he confessed, "I grew weak in the knees at near accidents. A Curtiss flyer, Beachy, dived 2,000 feet, but, as his machine didn't break, he was saved." Lincoln Beachy tried stunts more cautious airmen avoided; he once flew his plane under the Suspension Bridge at Niagara Falls.

The dangers of flying were obvious; the first day of the meet five machines crashed. On Monday, August 14, a biplane struck a power cable and was destroyed by fire. One aviator plummeted to the shores of Lake Michigan; two others splashed down in the lake itself. St. Croix Johnstone nosedived six hundred feet and was killed.

Houdini met Orville Wright and Glenn Hammond Curtiss. These famous airmen thought the first man to fly in Australia was an Australian and, Houdini wrote, "wanted to know all about my country."

Houdini did not exhibit his Voisin at the Chicago air meet. The year before he had crated it and taken it to England, where it was stored. He volunteered to participate in a hastily arranged benefit exhibition, staged the day after the meet ended, for the widow of St. Croix Johnstone. Manacled, he jumped from a plane as it flew fifty feet above Lake Michigan. Releasing himself underwater, he swam ashore.

Houdini never flew his Voisin again. The plane was acquired by Donald Stevenson, one of his wealthy English friends, for little more than the accumulated storage charges. Stevenson, in turn, sold it to another aviation enthusiast. Beyond that, no one knows what happened to the flying machine that, as a New Zealand paper stressed, brought Houdini a larger share of public notice "than even Andrew Fisher, the new Labour Premier of the Commonwealth."

Houdini summed up his achievement in more dramatic terms. He had, he told an Australian reporter, "conquered the four elements—fire, water, earth and air. Fire—when I leaped handcuffed and manacled into boiling malt—be sure I did not stay there long! Water—when I leaped handcuffed and manacled into icy rivers, where it was death if I missed my dive—death if I could not get free. Earth—night after night, mastering the resistance of matter to the flesh and the will. Air—when I made the first sustained flight on an aeroplane in Australia."

NELSON HARDING in THE BROOKLYN DAILY EAGLE
As an imitation of HOUDINI, it's awful

In *The Master Mystery*, a silent film serial, Houdini amazed
audiences by proving that he could use his toes like fingers.

4

The Film Maker

Houdini progressed from dime museums and circus sideshows to vaudeville. Then, during the final years of the First World War, when the motion picture began replacing the variety show, he prepared to make another transition. Conscious of his limited range as an actor, he firmly believed his daring escape feats could be effectively presented on the screen.

Producer B. A. Rolfe of Octagon Films signed the magician for a fifteen-part serial and hired Arthur B. Reeve and Charles A. Logue to write the scenario. They had already plotted such box-office successes as *The Perils of Pauline*, *The Clutching Hand*, and *The House of Hate*. Early in 1918, with Houdini as consultant, they began work on the script of *The Master Mystery*. The story line stressed suspense. Each episode ended with Houdini facing almost certain destruction. The scenario went like this:

Quentin Locke (Houdini), undercover agent for the United States Department of Justice, works as a chemist in the research laboratory of International Patents, Inc. This firm, secretly financed by powerful industrialists, purchases basic inventions solely to keep them off the market, thus saving its sponsors the vast sums they would have to spend retooling plants for improved products. Models of revolutionary engines, safety equipment, and communication devices are stored away in "the graveyard of inventions," a cavern beneath the mansion of Peter Brent. Brent, the president of Industrial Patents, Inc., has decided to reform. His partner, Herbert Balcom, is seeking to gain control of the firm by forcing Brent's lovely daughter, Eva, to marry Paul Balcom, his dissolute son.

To complicate matters, Eva Brent has fallen in love with Locke, the government investigator, and Paul Bascom enlists the aid of DeLuxe Dora, a sinister brunette. Peter Brent meanwhile receives threats from "Q," a mad scientist whose inventions have been suppressed, and from "The Automaton"—the screen's first robot villain.

The Automaton, described in advertisements as "three times the size of man," is not that gigantic. Still, with electric eyes and steel fingers from which lethal rays spark out, this monster terrified and delighted the youngsters who packed movie houses on Saturday matinees.

Locke braves assaults by the Automaton, a gang of thugs, an evil hypnotist, a Chinese Tong leader, a corrupt fortune-teller, and a strangulation expert from Madagascar. Locke makes daring leaps à la Douglas Fairbanks, opens a bolted door with a bent umbrella rib and a piece of string, and performs the same Houdini feats that thrilled vaudeville patrons—with harrowing variations to enhance the plot.

He releases himself from a straitjacket applied by the monster's minions.

Tied by his thumbs to the prongs of a wall hatrack, he clasps his legs in a scissorhold around the neck of an attacker and strangles him.

Then, without the aid of his hands, he removes a shoe and a stocking. Employing bare toes as agilely as fingers, he takes a key from the fallen thug's pocket, fits the key into a door, opens the door, and "walks up" the narrow edge. Reaching the top, he straddles the door, then unties his thumbs.

Fastened with manacles and leg-irons to a dock, Locke frees himself and pulls one of his attackers into the river, holding him at the bottom until he drowns, then slips from the restraints and surfaces.

Incarcerated in a jail cell adjacent to one occupied by a villain, Locke opens both doors, knocks out the thug, locks him into the first cell, then takes his place in the adjoining one.

Bound with rope and suspended head-down over a cauldron, Locke is to be lowered into seething acid the moment the unsuspecting heroine enters the room; the rope that holds him runs over a rafter and down to the door

Barbed wire, trickling acid, and other hazards added drama to the escapes in the serial.

Strapped to an electric chair, Houdini had to release himself or die by electrocution.

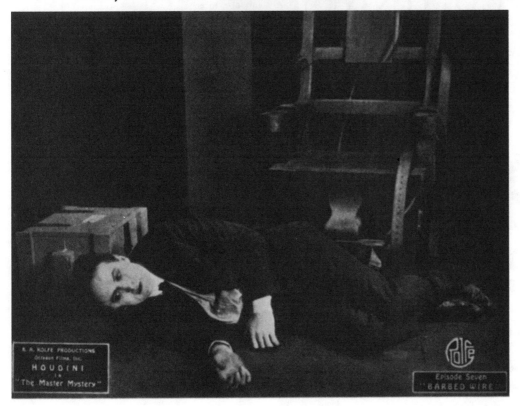

HOUDINI
THE HANDCUFF KING
WILL APPEAR IN

"The Master Mystery"

A story of love and intrigue by Arthur B. Reeve and Charles A. Logue.

Produced by
B. A. ROLFE

Left and *left below:* An advance advertisement describing the serial as a love story was not nearly as effective as others with imaginative illustrations.

This Is the Automaton!

¶ A mechanical figure with a human brain.

¶ A weird unconquerable villain.

¶ A metal masterpiece that cannot be destroyed.

¶ A giant form three times the size of a man.

¶ You see him in "The Master Mystery," featuring

HOUDINI

While the menacing Automaton was not "three times the size of a man," it delighted younger spectators.

COMING

"The Master Mystery"

FEATURING THE GREAT

HOUDINI
It's a super-story of thrills and excitement

HOUDINI

THE HANDCUFF KING
WILL APPEAR IN

"The Master Mystery"

A story of love and intrigue by Arthur B. Reeve and Charles A. Logue.

Produced by
B. A. ROLFE

Left and *left below:* An advance advertisement describing the serial as a love story was not nearly as effective as others with imaginative illustrations.

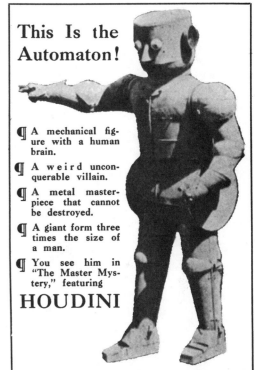

This Is the Automaton!

- A mechanical figure with a human brain.
- A weird unconquerable villain.
- A metal masterpiece that cannot be destroyed.
- A giant form three times the size of a man.
- You see him in "The Master Mystery," featuring

HOUDINI

While the menacing Automaton was not "three times the size of a man," it delighted younger spectators.

COMING

"The Master Mystery"

FEATURING THE GREAT

HOUDINI

It's a super-story of thrills and excitement

knob. Loosening one hand, Locke swings back and forth like a human pendulum until he can grasp the rafter. Then he pulls himself up and over the beam—just as the door opens.

Menaced by an assassin in a deep-sea diver's rig as he tests a similar suit with a safety-release feature, Locke dodges the attacker's knife. The blade slashes through the air hose to a pump in the boat above. Locke turns a knob; his helmet comes off and the weighted suit falls away. Unencumbered, he swims to the surface.

Nailed in a packing crate on a pier, the handcuffed Locke waves through a small hole in the side of the box as it is thrown overboard. Before the crate reaches the bottom, he is out and swimming away underwater.

In subsequent episodes the pace does not slacken.

Strapped to a "Chair of Death," with electrodes attached to the sides of his head and to the bare skin of his arms and legs, Locke breaks free a split second before a switch is thrown and bolts of electricity spark across the empty seat.

Secured to pipes in a huge empty storage tank on the roof of an apartment building, Locke struggles as water gushes over him. Freeing himself as the water level rises, he crawls over the ledge.

Wound in and bound by barbed wire on the basement floor of a cafe, he rolls away as rivulets of acid from an overturned cylinder seep toward his body. Then, lacerating his hands and arms on the sharp barbs, he wriggles free.

Thrown, after having been tied up, down an elevator shaft, Locke looks up to see the heavy elevator car inching down on its way to crush him. For once, prompt action by another person saves his life. An attractive young woman, who earlier has aided the opposition, throws her body against the control switch and brings the car to a sudden halt only fractions of an inch above his head.

Locke performs the most remarkable gymnastic feat in the serial after being shackled, hand and foot, to a wall. The ends of a rope encircling his neck run through the wall to a wheel. As a strangler from Madagascar turns the wheel, the rope tightens around Locke's neck. Locke slips from the shackles, then rapidly revolving his body like a giant hand on a mammoth clock, he spins around faster than the strangler can turn the wheel. Gaining slack, Locke pulls the loop over his head. (This preposterous release delighted movie fans.)

Hanging by the neck with his feet on a trapdoor in a Chinese temple, Locke releases his hands, reaches up, and takes a firm grip on the rope. Kicking at the wall behind him, he gains enough momentum to swing up until his leg can be hooked over a chandelier. Pulling himself up on the dangling light fixture, he unties the knots at his neck.

Each time the Automaton stalked into view, children at matinee performances shrieked and shouted.

Playing the role of an undercover investigator, Houdini discovers an important document.

The odds were always against Houdini in the melees with his screen adversaries.

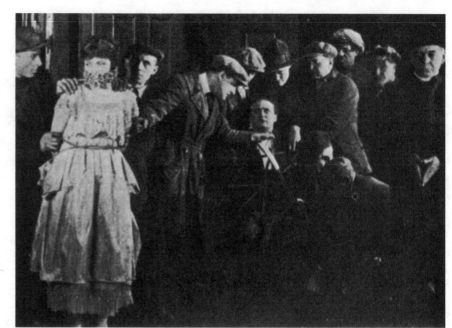

It was not difficult for the master escapologist to free himself after he had been tied to a chair.

To escape from a "strangling machine" was another matter. Trick photography heightened the excitement.

He slipped from the tightening noose only to be confronted again by the Automaton's minions.

Episodes of *The Master Mystery* ended with Houdini in a predicament with no apparent solution. Still, week after week, he survived.

For fourteen weeks he escaped from almost every sort of restraint.

Then, in the last episode, he admitted he had no wish to break from the bonds of marriage.

Buried beneath rocks and falling debris after an explosion, he kicks, claws, and digs his way up to fresh air.

Locke suspects that it was Herbert Balcom, Brent's partner in International Patents, Inc., who operated the Automaton from inside the hollow form. Since Balcom was killed when the building collapsed, the government agent believes his troubles with the steel monster are over.

Not so. The Automaton continues to menace him until Locke fells it with a newly invented gas-charged projectile. The robot's head is removed. Inside the monster is Balcom's son, Paul.

Silent movie serials, like fairy tales, always had a happy ending. Locke finally marries Eva Brent. When she expresses doubt that anything can hold him after his marvelous escapes, he smiles and turns his eyes toward the thin gold band on the third finger of her left hand.

Film-making had intrigued Houdini since his first visit to Paris in December 1901, when he had gone to the Théâtre Robert-Houdin to pay homage to the memory of the French magician he had idolized as a boy and from whom he had taken his stage name. Though the great innovator had died in 1871, many of his famous feats were still being performed there by the current proprietor, Georges Méliès.

To Houdini's surprise, short films produced by Méliès were featured more than the classical conjuring. The films, however, Houdini grudgingly admitted, merited top billing. Méliès with his camera magic was able to create illusions on the screen far more fantastic than any he could exhibit in person on the stage.

During a later engagement in Paris, Houdini appeared briefly in a film sequence filmed by Pathé. Roped to a chair, he struggles, frees himself, then thumbs his nose at the gendarme who has been guarding him.

Newsreel footage of Houdini's manacled leaps into rivers, filmed in Paris, Philadelphia, and Berlin, frequently preceded his vaudeville performances. Then, in 1910, pictures of his aerial exploits in Germany and his pioneering flights in Australia were added.

As technical consultant in 1916 to the Pathé thriller *The Mysteries of Myra*, Houdini devised a whirling-mirror hypnotism machine and special séance effects. A year later he wrote *The Marvelous Adventures of Houdini, the Justly Celebrated Elusive American* as a scenario for a possible feature film. B. A. Rolfe read this script soon after Houdini opened a nineteen-week run at the New York Hippodrome in January 1918. Rolfe thought that more money could be made with a serial. It was he who arranged plot conferences for Houdini with Arthur B. Reeve and Charles A. Logue.

Production of *The Mastery Mystery* began that spring in Yonkers, New York. Houdini told the press he wanted to record his escapes for posterity.

In *The Grim Game*, Houdini's first feature-length film, he again demonstrated his skill as an escapologist, and the publicity releases said, survived the first in-air plane collision ever recorded by a movie camera.

Betrayed by men he took to be his friends in *The Grim Game*, Houdini was arrested.

Only the heroine believed he was innocent, not guilty of an alleged murder.

Houdini has the last laugh on the belittling policemen who locked him in a cell.

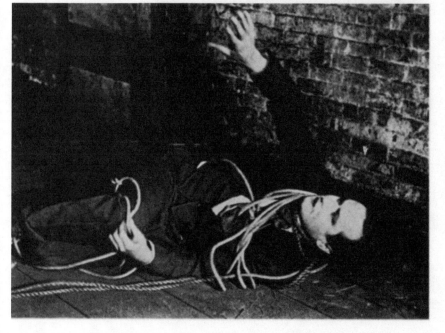

The elements of Houdini's feature-length films followed the pattern established by his serial. He fought against larger men, triumphed over the forces of evil.

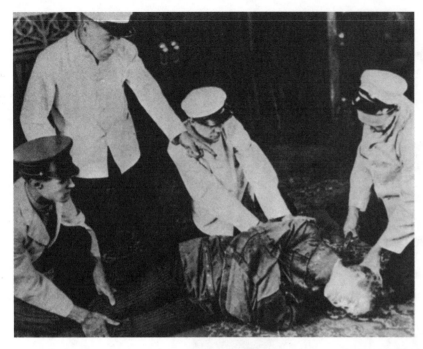

Houdini performed his own stunts in *The Master Mystery*. A double made the descent from one plane to another in *The Grim Game*.

Robert E. Kennedy, third man from the right, was doubling for Houdini as the planes crashed.

The scene with Houdini perched on the wing of a plane was shot in a Hollywood studio.

No double exposures or camera tricks were to be used in the serial. Despite this disclaimer, trick photography was used on occasion. Houdini's escape from the garroting machine, for example, was filmed by an overhead camera with the "wall" flat on the floor. He could scamper around in a circle with his neck in a noose while in this position, as he could not if the wall were upright.

A few months after *The Master Mystery* was released, Houdini signed a contract to make two feature films for Jesse A. Lasky and Paramount Art-craft Pictures in Hollywood. Arthur B. Reeve and John W. Grey collaborated on the script for *The Grim Game;* Irwin Willat directed, and Famous Players-Lasky Corporation distributed the finished product. In this film and the others that followed, the chief characters played by Houdini had names beginning with his initials—H. H. In *The Grim Game*, the hero was Harvey Hanford.

An out-of-favor nephew of eccentric millionaire Dudley Cameron, Hanford earns his living as star reporter of *The Call*. Though Hanford does not know it, three men are plotting against Cameron for as many reasons. His doctor hopes to get the old man's millions by marrying his ward, Mary. Richard Raver, Cameron's lawyer, has been illicitly transferring the millionaire's money to his personal bank account; aware of this, Cameron has threatened to have him jailed. Meanwhile, Clifton Allison, owner-publisher of *The Call*, has borrowed heavily from Cameron. The millionaire can put the newspaper out of business by calling in the short-term loans.

The three conspirators meet. Afterward the publisher asks the unsuspecting Hanford to participate in a sensational circulation-building stunt. The reporter, with help from the conniving publisher, will prove to the public that circumstantial evidence is not always valid. The first part is successfully carried out. Cameron's physician sends the financier to a remote hunting lodge "for his health" in the company of a beautiful night club entertainer who is posing as a nurse. The reporter slips past the guards of Cameron's mansion, upsets furniture, breaks objects, and makes it appear there has been a fight. He leaves obvious clues to his identity behind and is duly arrested.

In jail, Hanford to his dismay learns that the millionaire's body has been found in a well on the estate. Instead of the publisher breaking an exclusive story proving that the incriminating evidence has been planted, he denies any knowledge of his investigative reporter's activities.

Only one person believes Hanford is innocent—the girl he loves, Cameron's ward, Mary. Hanford sends her to the hunting lodge in an attempt to get a confession from the "nurse." Meanwhile, Cameron's doctor arranges for Hanford to be committed to an asylum.

JESSE L. LASKY PRESENTS

HOUDINI
in
"THE GRIM GAME"

By ARTHUR B. REEVE and JOHN W. GRAY
Directed by IRVIN WILLAT

HERE'S HOW IT HAPPENED

On June first, 1919, the Associated Press carried from Los Angeles a story of the thrilling aeroplane accident that took place during the filming of "The Grim Game." The story of the two planes which crashed together in mid-air and plunged to earth buzzed on the wires to every newspaper in America.

You will see that collision in "The Grim Game." It was an accident, but the camera man had the presence of mind to keep it turning.

The drawings on this page show how it happened.

Houdini on the rope attempts to descend to the lower plane. The camera man was in the third machine.

The lower machine turned its propeller upward — the propellers gnashed together —

The lower plane crashed into the upper one — cutting off a wing —

The two planes, locked and helpless, crashed to earth!

It's all in the picture — and lots more! The greatest thrill in the greatest thrill picture ever made!

FAMOUS PLAYERS~LASKY CORPORATION
ADOLPH ZUKOR *Pres.* JESSE L. LASKY *Vice Pres.* CECIL B. DE MILLE *Director General*
NEW YORK.

A Paramount Artcraft Picture

CAMERA MAN

The reporter breaks from his padded cell, is captured on the roof of the building, and strapped in a straitjacket. Releasing himself while suspended upside-down over the street, he falls to the top of an awning, then jumps to the pavement.

Commandeering a *Call* airplane, he is flown to a landing strip near the Cameron lodge, with the publisher following him in another plane. Eluding guards on the wilderness estate, Hanford steps into the noose of a bear trap and is yanked high in the air. Freeing himself, he runs to the lodge, where the three conspirators try to capture him. During this fight, the publisher shoots the doctor. The lawyer, appalled by this violence, confesses that he was in the Cameron mansion the night the millionaire was slain. He had planned to rob the safe, and he saw the publisher fire the bullet that killed Cameron.

The publisher flees in his plane, with the reporter following in another. Hanford's plane climbs above the publisher's; then the reporter lashes a rope to a wing and starts down to the plane below. Suddenly—at an altitude of 3,000 feet—the planes collide, spiral toward the ground, and crash.

This thrilling sequence was not in the original script, but Director Willat, in a third plane, had filmed the accident. Wire-service stories reported Houdini escaped with minor injuries from this brush with death. Though the planes were shattered, no one was killed. Actually, Houdini was not in the air at the time of the collision. He had fractured his wrist in an earlier scene. Lieutenant Robert E. Kennedy, a stunt man, had doubled for him. This fact the Paramount-Artcraft publicity department suppressed.

With the story rewritten to include the accident, the wing-to-wing descent made by Houdini was filmed in a studio. That another man had taken his place in the air was one of the escapologist's best-kept secrets.

After *The Grim Game* opened in New York, *Morning Telegraph* reviewer Agnes Smith said:

> Audiences know Houdini, and they know that if he appears to fool them, he is doing it honestly. Therefore, they knew that when they saw him (in the picture) extricate himself from shackles, get out of a detention suit while suspended head downward, and leap under a speeding truck, that he was doing these things by his own skill and not by the aid of a clever cameraman.

The *New York Herald* critic, Harriet Underhill, praised both *The Grim Game* and its star: "Combining dare-deviltry with his familiar wizardry in getting out of tight places, Houdini, escape artist, has stepped to the front as a film star. . . . The picture is one of the best of recent Broadway offerings."

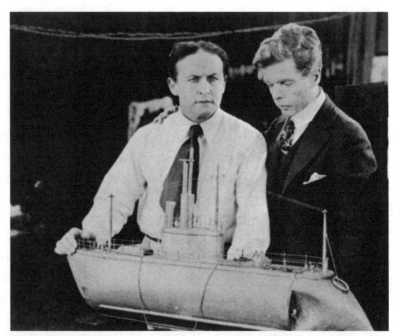

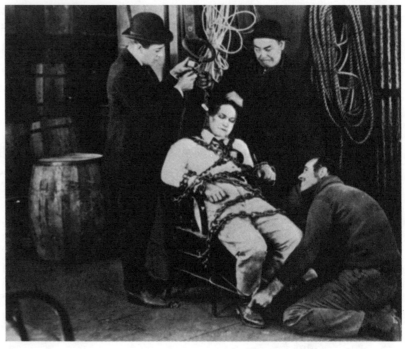

Houdini being attacked by cannibals in *Terror Island*. He escapes from being roasted alive in one exciting sequence.

With a model of the super-submarine that took him to "the remote island in the Pacific Ocean."

Before he could make the journey, Houdini had to outwit his adversaries.

Star, cast, director, and crew
on location, Catalina Island.

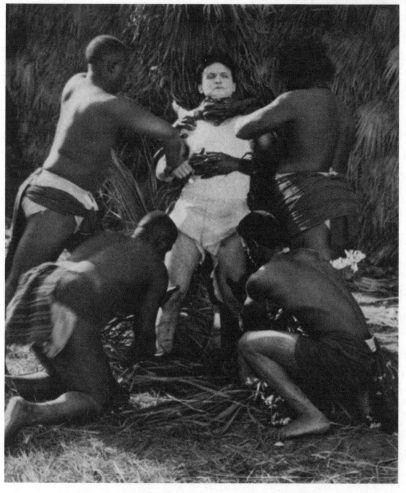

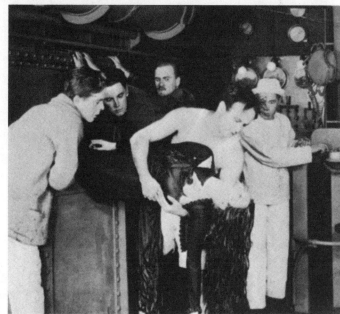

Inside the submarine, following
Houdini's rescue of the heroine from
a submerged safe.

Note the indentation on the left
thigh. This remainder of an old
injury was erroneously thought by
some people to be a "skin pocket,"
used to conceal escape tools.

Terror Island, Houdini's second film for Lasky, produced in Hollywood in the fall of 1919, offered him the opportunity to triumph over cannibals. Location shots were made on Catalina Island, but most of the action was filmed on the California mainland.

Harry Harper (Houdini), a wealthy San Francisco philanthropist and sportsman, invents a supersubmarine. Beverly West comes to him with the news that her father is being held by savages on Terror Island, a remote Pacific isle. Unless she returns the sacred pearl her father has sent her, he will be the main course on the tribe's next feast day.

In the wreckage of a ship near the island, Beverly says, there is a safe filled with diamonds. She and Harper will be able both to rescue her father and acquire a fortune. Unfortunately, her conniving uncle, his son, and an unprincipled buccaneer are aware of the situation. They break into Harper's mansion, fell him with a steel pipe, then bind him to a chair. They attach a string to the bell on the telephone and extend it to a burning candle, balanced precariously on a sheaf of gasoline-soaked papers, adjacent to a box of blasting powder. When the phone rings, the string will dislodge the candle; the incendiary papers will ignite, and the lethal powder explode.

Regaining consciousness, Harper struggles with his bonds. The phone rings briefly. Just enough to make the candle wobble. The phone rings again—longer. The lighted candle topples over; the papers start to burn. The fire is about to trigger an explosion when Harper frees his hands and hurls aside the box of blasting powder.

Later, after escaping from a submerged crate, Harper embarks in his submarine in an effort to rescue Beverly, who has been kidnapped by her relatives and is being taken to Terror Island on their ship. The submarine catches up with the vessel, Harper boards it, fights off the crew, and dives from the deck with Beverly. They swim together underwater to the submarine.

Beverly's father is about to be roasted alive on Terror Island when Harper disrupts the precooking rites. He gives the sacred pearl to the chieftain. The ungracious cannibal changes the menu, binding Harper to the grid. Beverly, who has accompanied him, is to be disposed of in a different way. Locked with the diamonds in the safe recovered from the wrecked ship, she is taken by tribesmen to a high cliff.

Harper struggles free and runs after the procession, dodging spears along the way. He watches in horror as the safe rolls off the cliff and into the sea. He dives after it. On the ocean floor he works against time to get the right combination and open the safe before Beverly suffocates. He turns the lever; the heavy door moves forward, and Beverly emerges. Pausing only to scoop up the diamonds, Harper swims with Beverly to the waiting submarine. Soon they are heading back to San Francisco Bay.

HOUDINI

IN "The MAN FROM BEYOND"

CHALLENGE

I, HARRY HOUDINI, hereby challenge any producer in the world, and am willing to forfeit $5,000 to any one who can produce upon the screen a greater thrill than the Rescue Scene at the Brink of Niagara Falls in my new photodrama, "The Man From Beyond."

"The Man From Beyond" has the greatest thrill ever depicted on stage or screen.

Houdini plunges into the raging water of Niagara, in a desperate effort to save the girl who has leaped into a frail canoe rather than fall into the clutches of the villain.

The canoe with its precious burden is tossed about in the tempestuous waters with Houdini, swept among the rocks in the swift current, in its wake.

He seizes the canoe, stops it, only to have it wrested from his grasp by the raging torrent. He reaches it again at the very brink of the roaring cataract of Niagara Falls. Once more occurs a desperate struggle to save the girl—a struggle that for excitement and thrills excels all the rescue scenes of all times.

Besides this there are other thrills, all woven into the haunting, romantic story of a man who is chopped out of his icy tomb in the Arctics after one hundred years to be brought back to life.

THEATRE NAME

The story of a man found frozen in a mass of Arctic ice who upon being chopped out is brought back to life to live the most haunting romance ever told and ending with the greatest thrill ever screened —Houdini's rescue of the girl on the very brink of Niagara Falls.

NOTE — This picture comes direct from its sensational run at the New York Times Square Theatre, at $2.00 prices

PRODUCED BY HOUDINI PICTURE CORP.

HOUDINI

"The MAN FROM BEYOND"

Reincarnation was the theme of *The Man From Beyond*. Critics acclaimed the brink-of-Niagara-Falls rescue.

HOUDINI

in

"The MAN FROM BEYOND"

Here's the weirdest, most uncanny, yet the most fascinating picture ever screened.

It tells a haunting romance—the story of a man who, after being frozen in a mass of Arctic ice for 100 years, is chopped out and returned to civilization to meet his reincarnated love of a century before.

And thrills! They crowd one upon the other reaching their climax in the rescue of the girl by Houdini on the very brink of Niagara Falls.

Positively the most daring rescue scene ever screened.

HOUDINI in "THE MAN FROM BEYOND"

The weirdest and most sensational love story ever told on the screen—a man encased in the heart of a glacier of ice for 100 years, upon being hewn out comes back to life to live a romance of haunting charm, reaching its climax in the greatest thrill ever depicted.

SEE HOUDINI WHIRLED TO THE BRINK OF NIAGARA FALLS TO RESCUE THE GIRL

HOUDINI in

THRILLS!
ROMANCE!
MYSTERY!

Direct from sensational run at Times Square Theatre, New York, at $2 prices.

"Never a spectacle so impressive."
—N. Y. *Eve. Journal*

"One of the most startling photoplay views ever made."
—N. Y. *World*

"As honestly exciting a moment as one could have."—N. Y. *Herald*

"Idea certainly novel one. Strikingly daring feat."—N. Y. *Eve. Mail*

"Interesting stuff. Fantastic conception."
—N. Y. *Times*

"Weird, interesting, startling."
—N. Y. *Eve. Post*

"The MAN FROM BEYOND"

An opening "Arctic" sequence was made in part at Lake Placid. Houdini wrote, produced, and starred in the production.

Seaman Houdini aboard a
vessel that was to be frozen in
the Arctic for a hundred years.

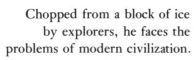

Chopped from a block of ice
by explorers, he faces the
problems of modern civilization.

Houdini, cameramen, actors, and technicians relax on shipboard. For him this was a real accomplishment; he could get seasick just looking at a boat in a harbor.

The president of the Houdini Picture Corporation and his staff at Niagara Falls.

Cecil B. DeMille had suggested this approach to a buzz saw one day in Hollywood.

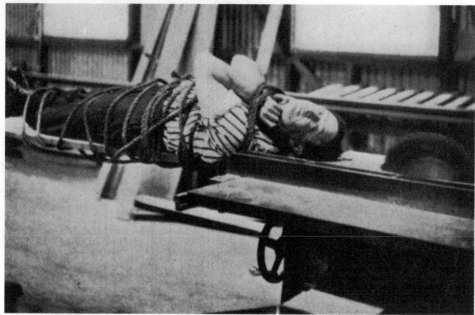

Neither *Terror Island* nor *The Grim Game* was as profitable for Houdini as *The Master Mystery* had been. His contract for the serial called for an advance payment of $20,000, plus half the net earnings. A year after the series was released, Houdini sued for his share of the profits. He claimed $32,795.19 was due him. He won the case and was awarded precisely that amount. By then the worldwide profits had soared to $250,000; he filed another suit for his portion of this bonanza.

Though motion pictures were now his major interest, Houdini sailed for England in late December 1919 to fill the vaudeville contracts that had been postponed by the First World War and to film outdoor scenes on location for future projects. He had enjoyed, for the most part, his association with Jesse Lasky, but thought he was better qualified than the Paramount-Artcraft producer to have the final say on scripts and production details.

The success of the six-month tour abroad seemed to confirm this judgment. He set up the Houdini Picture Corporation and in ten days wrote the story for *The Man from Beyond*, his next feature film. He named himself president and producer and hired Burton King, who had directed *The Master Mystery*, to work as advertisements later said, "Under the supervision of Houdini." Coolidge Streeter adapted Houdini's story for the screen with the magician as an active collaborator. The script had the most imaginative sequences yet.

Howard Hillary (Houdini), frozen for a hundred years on a ship in the Arctic, revives after being chopped from a block of ice by explorers. Recovering from his state of suspended animation, Hillary's first thought is of Felice, the girl he loved at the time of the shipwreck. Returning to civilization, the men visit the home of Professor Strange, a brother of one of the explorers, near Niagara Falls. Strange's daughter, Felice, who is about to be married to Dr. Gilbert Trent, looks exactly like the girl Hillary was parted from a century earlier. Hillary, not yet realizing how long he has been frozen, thinks she is the same girl, and rushes forward to claim her. Dr. Trent, furious because the wedding ceremony is delayed, has Hillary committed to a mental hospital. Rolled in sheets, tied, then locked in a cell as water pours down on him from above, Hillary nonetheless manages to wriggle loose and climb out of the cell through an opening in the ceiling. He carefully knots the sheets end to end and uses them as a rope to let himself down from the top of the institution's high wall.

Rushing back to the Strange estate, he scales the outside of the mansion and climbs in through Felice's bedroom window. She listens sympathetically to his tale of a shipboard romance, then points to the date on a newspaper—1920! For the first time Hillary understands how much time has gone by. For her part, the professor's daughter wonders if she is the reincarnation of the earlier Felice.

While in Hollywood, Houdini visited with Professor Harry G. Cooke, president of the Los Angeles Society of Magicians.

Retired illusionist Harry Kellar gave Houdini the "Psycho" he had presented for years in his show. Houdini hoped to write a Kellar biography. It was not completed.

Her fiancé, Dr. Trent, and Marie LeGrande (played by Nita Naldi, one of the most popular vamps of the silent films) conspire to have Hillary accused of murdering Professor Strange, Felice's now-missing father. Strange, meanwhile, is Trent's prisoner in a dungeon. The doctor lures Felice to his remote laboratory, intending to drug her and force her to marry him.

Hillary tracks Felice to the lab, fights with Trent, while she flees, with one of the doctor's cohorts following close behind her. Hillary and Trent, exchanging blows, move to a ledge above a canyon. Hillary slips and falls, clinging to the ledge with his fingers. Trent tries to dislodge his grip, but Hillary, securing a foothold, mounts to the top of the lofty rock and tosses Trent into the ravine.

Trying to elude her pursuer, Felice rushes to the banks of the rapids above Niagara Falls, and leaps into a canoe. The swift current carries her toward the swirling falls. Hillary swims after her. Long shots of the thundering falls and closeups of her terrified expressions quicken moviegoers' pulsebeats. Moments before the canoe is swept over the brink, Hillary reaches Felice, throws one arm around her, then makes for the shore.

This scene alone was worth the price of admission, critics said, when *The Man from Beyond* opened at the Times Square Theatre on Broadway in April 1922. To insure full houses for the three-week engagement, Houdini appeared in person, presenting an elaborate stage show.

This combination of live and screen entertainment paid off. Houdini also boosted the box-office take of the film in Washington, Detroit, and Buffalo with personal appearances, and sent out three units made up of magicians, mind readers, and escapologists to appear with the motion picture in other cities.

Houdini's friend, Sir Arthur Conan Doyle, then in the United States for a lecture tour, gave the film his personal endorsement: "I have no hesitation in saying it is the very best sensational picture I have ever seen. . . . it holds one breathless. I consider *The Man from Beyond* one of the really great contributions to the screen."

Haldane of the Secret Service, the second feature film of the Houdini Picture Corporation, was like the first one based on a story written by the producer-star.

Heath Haldane, Jr. (Houdini), the secret-agent son of a government investigator who was murdered by international counterfeiters, fights off a gang that attacks Adele Ormsby on a New York street. He picks up a satchel filled with fake bank notes dropped by a gang member and escorts Adele home. There he learns her father has been an attaché at an American

HOUDINI

WORLD FAMOUS HANDCUFF KING

IN HALDANE OF THE SECRET SERVICE

STRAPPED to a whirling wheel of death, tons of water rushing over him, it didn't seem possible that even Houdini could escape from this last desperate plot of the counterfeiters!

But Houdini does escape and the manner in which he does it adds just one more to the hundreds of thrills in which this picture abounds.

Talk about action! Every second is jammed with it—red-blooded, plausible action—and it builds right up to a climax that will take your breath away with amazement!

Don't whatever you do, miss this entertainment special!

With GLADYS LESLIE and All-Star Cast

The second and final film made by the Houdini Film Corporation did not compare with the first.

embassy in China and that the counterfeiters distributed the sham bills from abroad in an old warehouse on the Hudson River docks. He opens the satchel. The fake bank notes have vanished. Someone in the Ormsby home has switched satchels.

Detected while spying on the gang at the warehouse, Haldane is overpowered, tied up, and thrown into the river. Rescued by the crew of a tugboat, Haldane swims from it to the liner *Aquitania,* then leaving the harbor for Britain. Uncovering evidence in Hull and London that the spurious bank notes came from France, the secret-service agent goes to Paris. After a brawl in an Apache café, he locates the source of the supply in an old monastery in a remote village. Garbed as monks, and working for Dr. Ku, a Chinese mastermind, the counterfeiters operate a printing press in a concealed room beneath the chapel.

Captured, then bound to the side of a huge waterwheel, Haldane releases himself as the wheel turns and he is about to be crushed. Unmasking Dr. Ku as Adele's father, Haldane completes his mission and, knowing she has not been part of the gang, asks her to be his bride.

Lacking the sensational elements of his previous films, *Haldane of the Secret Service* was a box-office disaster. Houdini had underestimated production costs, spliced in footage shot on his 1920 British tour, and neglected to make proper arrangements for the distribution of either this or his *Man from Beyond.* The business side of film-making bored him; he abhorred the routine paperwork. He lost money with the Houdini Picture Corporation and with a film-developing plant he had set up in New Jersey with his brother Hardeen as the supervisor. On the plus side, Houdini's vaudeville salary soared to $3,000 a week, and people in parts of the world he had never visited now knew him not only as a master escapologist but as a film star.

Some of the more persistent fables about Houdini's career can be traced to the press material sent to exhibitors to publicize his movies. The brochure for *The Master Mystery* said that he had escaped from Siberian dungeons "and in the Orient tabernacles were built to his prowess." Furthermore, while performing in "the interiors of China and Japan," he traveled "in a huge motor car" that "opened to six times its own length and had a seating capacity of five hundred." While Houdini had made a trip around the world, he had never visited or performed in any of the areas mentioned.

When he was a boy, his mother did not apprentice him to a locksmith in Wisconsin nor did he ever throw himself across a railway track when a conductor refused to load his trunks on a train. He never labored two hours trying to escape from "a certain British prison" only to discover that the cell door had not been locked.

Neither Houdini nor Gladys Leslie was in good form in *Haldane of the Secret Service*.

The romantic scenes were obviously a chore for the hero and his leading lady.

Even the big waterwheel escape lacked impact on the screen.

The man with the cigar is Burton King, director of *The Master Mystery* and *The Man From Beyond*.

The press book for *The Grim Game* quoted Houdini, the scourge of psychic charlatans, as saying, "I do not think we return to earth after death in the bodies of cats or other dumb animals. But I do firmly believe that we somehow come back to carry on, as it were, through another lifetime, perhaps through many succeeding lifetimes, until our allotted destiny is worked out to its ultimate solution." The theme of *The Grim Game* was, of course, reincarnation.

The Man from Beyond press book sought to make his pioneering airplane flights in Australia even more historic by claiming he "was one of the thirty original airmen of the world." Aviation records indicate Houdini was more likely one of the first thousand aviators.

Any doubt as to how his name should be pronounced was removed by a quotation from the 1920 edition of Funk & Wagnalls' *New Standard Dictionary*—"Hoo-dee-nee." Later editions note that the accent is on the second syllable. Only the most famous of the famous rate a dictionary entry while they are still alive. Houdini's name has since been added to other dictionaries, and his biography appears in encyclopedias.

Though not as important in cinema history as his illusionist predecessor Georges Méliès or the present-day actor, producer, magician Orson Welles, Houdini is still remembered in the movie capital of the world. On October 31, 1975, a bronze marker was inserted with traditional fanfare in the pavement of Hollywood Boulevard—"the Street of the Stars"—near the Orange Drive intersection, honoring the versatile performer whose amazing feats thrilled cinema patrons years before the movies learned how to talk.

P.H. *in* BERLINER ULK, BERLIN GERMANY

Vor der Polizei hat er eine Gratisvorstellung gegeben, aber die wirklich von ihm was lernen können, müssen sich das Geld dazu förmlich stehlen.

(FREE TRANSLATION)
Houdini gives a performance free for the police but those who really want to take advantage of Houdini's knowledge must steal the money

Sir Arthur Conan Doyle invited Houdini to lunch in London in
1920. Their views on Spiritualism clashed, but for several years
they were the best of friends.

5

Conan Doyle and the Spirits

Long before Houdini met Sir Arthur Conan Doyle, he wrote a letter to Sherlock Holmes, the British author's famous detective. "Characterless men," the letter read, had taken names similar to his, and were stealing "the fruits of my brain work, and years of research for new tricks." They had broken into his trunks backstage at the Circus Busch in Berlin, and had tried to bribe his loyal assistant, Franz Kukol. "They are trying to get rid of me, by either crippling me for life or even going to the extreme of taking my life in cold blood." Houdini implored his "Dear Friend" to come to Germany immediately and aid in the fight against these criminals.

Houdini had no intention of mailing this letter. It appeared as an illustration in *Der Kettensprenger Houdini und der Welt-Detektif*, an anonymously written paperback thriller published in Berlin in December 1908. According

Houdini knew more about mediumistic tricks than most investigators. At one period, he and his wife posed as psychics.

to the story, Holmes crossed the channel, took a train to the German capital, and soon had the criminals behind bars.

It is most unlikely that Sir Arthur Conan Doyle knew about this adventure of his Baker Street sleuth when he wrote to Houdini on March 15, 1920, to thank him for a favor. Learning that Sir Arthur was searching for data concerning the Davenport Brothers, two American stage mediums who had been the center of a bitter controversy in England in 1864, the magician had mailed him a copy of his own book, which had bearing on the subject.

This volume, *The Unmasking of Robert-Houdin*, an attack by Houdini on the French magician he once idolized, charged that the "father of modern magic" had pirated some of his outstanding feats from earlier conjurers. Actually, while these tricks and illusions seemed to be the same as those featured by Robert-Houdin's predecessors, he had enhanced them, either with new methods or superior presentations. In later life, Houdini admitted to close friends that he should have presented his material—information about notable performers of the past and intriguing illustrations—as a history. The biased attempt to downgrade the man from whom he had taken his stage name had its origin in Paris; the ailing elderly widow of one of Robert-Houdin's sons had refused to talk with the brash escape artist.

Houdini was sure that the pages he had devoted to the Davenport Brothers would interest Conan Doyle. The American mediums had been securely tied to plank seats inside a large wooden cabinet. Musical instruments hanging near them played almost as soon as the doors were closed. "They fairly startled the world with their so-called manifestations of spiritualism," Houdini said, explaining that "the two men slipped in and out of the ropes without delay."

Robert-Houdin had not been an escape artist; his theory was that the Davenports released themselves by compressing their hands until they were practically the same size in diameter as their wrists. Houdini took delight in pointing out: "I have gone so far as to have iron bands made and press my hands together, hoping eventually to make my hands smaller than my wrists, but this has failed. . . . Even if the entire thumb were cut away, I believe it would still be impossible to slip a rope that was properly bound around the wrist."

Amused to find one magician disagreeing with another about mediumistic methods, Doyle, a firm believer in psychical phenomena, said in his letter of acknowledgment that he personally was not convinced that the Davenports had ever "really" been exposed. He added a postscript: "Some of our people think that you have yourself some psychic power, but I feel it is art and practice."

One of Sir Arthur's friends, J. Hewat McKenzie, president of the British College of Psychic Science, stated unequivocally in his book *Spirit Intercourse, Its Theory and Practice*, published in London in 1916, that Houdini "has for years demonstrated dematerialization, and the passage of matter through matter upon the public stage." The escape artist's "psychic power," McKenzie insisted, enabled him "to open any lock, handcuff, or bolt that is submitted to him."

When Doyle met Houdini in April 1920, they became friends, though their views on psychic phenomena clashed. The skeptic told the believer—as he did the public at every performance—that he accomplished his marvels solely by natural means. Further, Ira Davenport had demonstrated to him how he gained enough slack to release his hands during the cabinet séances.

Doyle had been "so impressed" by Houdini's vaudeville act, the magician noted, that "there is little wonder in his believing in Spiritualism so implicitly."

Unfamiliar with methods of trickery, Sir Arthur decided that despite Houdini's disavowal of mediumistic ability, he must have a "wonderful power." By late June when Doyle learned the American had been attending séances with a group from the Society for Psychical Research, he wrote, "Why do they never think of investigating you?"

Through Doyle, Houdini gained entry to many séance rooms where otherwise he would not have been welcome. He never attempted to disrupt the sittings, and he failed to find a medium who convinced him: "The more I investigate the subject, the less I can make myself believe."

On six occasions, Doyle said, he talked with his dead son "face to face."

Twice he thought his dead brother materialized, and once a dead nephew seemed to appear. He was positive William Hope, a spirit photographer, took pictures of the dead, and he accepted two snapshots, made by a little girl, of four fairies and a goblin in a Yorkshire forest as authentic. He said in a letter to the magician that undoubtedly Houdini would brand the woodland photographs fakes, but to him they were a revelation.

Among the mediums that Doyle suggested Houdini should visit was Etta Wriedt. Some sitters claimed she could produce three different spirit voices at once. On occasion, as she sat in the dark, barking dogs were heard and misty forms appeared. Mrs. Wriedt lived in Detroit, but made periodic trips to Britain. Houdini learned when he went to see her in London that she had crossed on the same ship that brought him to England. He sat in her séance room for an hour. Nothing happened. He thought she must be afraid of him.

Doyle verified this suspicion less than two weeks later when the medium came to his home. Sir Arthur assured her Houdini was a sincere searcher for the truth. She gave a séance for the author, his wife, and his secretary. As the four sang hymns together, a fifth voice was heard. The séance was held in the family nursery. How could there have been any deception? Doyle asked the magician.

Knowing his friend could not be swayed, Houdini did not discuss the issue. He did, however, speak of his firsthand knowledge of spirit fraud.

In the late 1890's, before Houdini had been booked on the Orpheum Circuit, he and his wife had posed as mediums. He gathered information about their clients by listening to small-town gossip, and making notes of names and dates on tombstones in churchyards. While probing for data in Wilmington, Delaware, he had learned about an unsuspected murder. This, he said, without giving further details, was one of several reasons why he returned to more honorable endeavors. He was trying to atone for the fraud he had practiced as a foolish young man by exposing the ruses of Hatfield Pettibone, a charlatan who had preyed on the bereaved for many months in St. Joseph, Missouri.

An undated clipping, now in the Christopher Collection, headed "HOUDINI'S EXPOSÉ—The Juggler Shows How Mediums Perform Their Tricks," tells of Houdini's first performance as an uncoverer of mediumistic deceptions.

Three chairs were placed on the platform directly in front of a medium's cabinet. The cabinet's curtains were closed. Three windowlike openings had earlier been cut in the curtains. Two volunteers from the audience sat in adjacent chairs at the left and center; Houdini took the one at the right. He explained, as Pettibone had done, that the man in the center was

Will Goldston (*to the left below*) endorsed
Spiritualism; Harry Blackstone (*with Houdini to
the right*) said it was "bunk."

Other famous mystifiers agreed with
Blackstone. Among them, Stuart Cumberland
(*center above*) and Servais Le Roy (*between
Houdini and Blackstone to the right*).

Medium (*extreme right*) puts her hands on a volunteer's arm, as does a spectator on the left.

A cloth is draped over the bodies of the participants. Almost at once manifestations begin.

How? Pressure on the arm from the medium's thumb as well as her fingers permits her to utilize her right hand undetected. This technique was perfected by the Eddy family.

to generate power for the spirits. He told him to put his hands on his knees. The other volunteer, also following instructions, grasped the man's right arm with both his hands; Houdini gripped the left arm in the same way.

Mrs. Houdini covered the three men with a large cloth so that only their heads were visible. A photographer named Banning brought his chair to the platform, sat with his back toward the audience, and grasped the hands of the man in the center through the cloth, just as Mrs. Pettibone, the medium's wife, had done during her husband's séances.

Soon ghostly hands waved out through the openings in the cabinet's curtains. Then Mrs. Houdini dramatically pulled away the cloth that had hidden the participants' bodies. One of Houdini's hands was free. He had reached back through the parting in the curtains of the cabinet to thrust his hand up and out first from one opening and then another.

In this technique, which was perfected by the Eddy family in Vermont, the medium closes his left hand around the arm of the volunteer in the center, extending the thumb parallel to the arm. His right hand covers this thumb. Once the cloth is in place, the medium can remove his right hand without detection as his left thumb continues to press down on the volunteer's arm. After the materializations, the right hand returns to its former position.

A woman in the audience questioned Houdini about the spirit writing Pettibone produced on blank slates. Once your hand is free, the magician answered, it can be used to write, as well as to wave.

Converts were made, Houdini continued, by giving confirmable messages. Again playing the role of Pettibone, he concentrated, then reeled off several incidents from someone's past.

To quote from the St. Joseph newspaper:

> Houdini asked if there was any man in the audience whose history had been told. There was a silence and Houdini asked if Mr. McSpadden was present.
>
> "Is it not truth that I have told," asked Houdini. The gentleman called upon admitted it was, and he was much puzzled at Houdini's knowledge.
>
> "There is nothing strange about that [the magician asserted]. I simply wished to show how easy it is to become possessed of a person's past history."

Houdini told Conan Doyle that Pettibone's supporters had tried to stop this exposure, "but the show went on."

Another medium named Baynes had a séance room in St. Joseph near the public library; he hired an old man who knew many of the people in town as a researcher. When this man spotted familiar faces entering the séance room, he would hustle over to the library. From city directories, he copied down addresses—and the names of relatives—then conveyed the information to Baynes.

Cecilia Weiss and Houdini,
who adored her. He dropped
unconscious to the floor at the
news of her death.

Bess Houdini with her arm
around Mrs. Weiss. Bess's
mother is at the left.
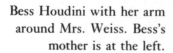

TO MY MOTHER.

"AMA!"
The first sound all babies coo!
"Mother!"
The first word all babies speak!
"Mama!" Such a sacred word that, in all languages of the world, it is spelled and pronounced alike.

No matter what rank you hold, what wealth you possess, whether King or Queen, citizen or knave, but one Mother is the lot of each.

This Mother, to whom Eternity means no more than a fleeting, forgotten second of Time, when working or watching for her children, you must cherish while she is with you so that, when the pitiless Reaper brings from the Almighty the Mandate recalling Mother, you may receive from your ever-present Conscience the consolation coming from the knowledge that you tried to smooth, tried to remove, the briers from the path which she trod through this Mortal Valley of the shadow of Death.

The poet who wrote "God Himself could not be Everywhere so He made Mothers" - gives poetic utterance to my own sentiment.

HARRY HOUDINI.

Tribute to his mother written by Houdini.

Another photograph taken the
same day as the one above.

Until Houdini's mother died, he seldom thought about the possibility of authentic messages from the dead; afterward, he consulted many mediums on the off-chance that he could reach her. Willing to concede there might be genuine psychics among the frauds, he had welcomed the guidance he received from Sir Arthur in England, though he became as sorely disappointed by British mediums as he was by their American counterparts.

Doyle came to the United States to lecture in 1922. Spiritualism was a fact, the gentle-voiced author stated. Skeptics disputed this statement, saying Spiritualism had not been proved scientifically. "I don't need scientific proof of what I heard with my own ears, see with my own eyes," Sir Arthur replied. When they met again, Houdini reminded his friend that the sense of sight and the sense of hearing are the most readily deceived.

Houdini and his wife were in the audience when Doyle spoke in New York at Carnegie Hall. The Doyles came to see Houdini's film *The Man from Beyond* at the Times Square Theatre. They were also his guests at the annual banquet of the Society of American Magicians.

In Washington, Doyle endorsed the Zancigs, a telepathy team: "Their performance as I saw it, was due to psychic causes (thought transference) and not to trickery." Houdini was appalled at the gullibility of his friend. Julius Zancig was a member of the Society of American Magicians; Houdini had purchased from him the ingenious code Zancig used to send information secretly to his partner.

Hoping to give Sir Arthur an object lesson, Houdini invited his friend and B. M. L. Ernst, the magician's lawyer, to his home. Ernst later told of the encounter in *Houdini and Conan Doyle*.

Houdini exhibited a slate, about fifteen inches high and eighteen inches long, with wires fastened to the upper corners. He told Doyle to hang it by the wires on one side of his library. Then he showed Doyle four small cork balls on a saucer and told him to choose two; the first would be sliced in half, so it could be thoroughly examined. Sir Arthur picked one; Houdini cut it open, and passed the pieces to Doyle. The second ball selected by the author, Houdini scooped up with a spoon and dropped into a well filled with white ink.

The magician then told his friend to leave the house, to walk away until he was out of sight of it in any direction, and then to write one or several words on a piece of paper. He was to fold the paper, put it in his pocket, and return. Doyle followed these instructions. Houdini invited him to take a spoon and remove the cork ball, which had been soaking in the white ink, then to touch the ball to the left side of the slate. The ball adhered. Slowly it began moving across the surface, writing "*Mene, mene, tekel, upharsin.*" These were the very words Doyle himself had written!

The believer and the doubter on the beach before the séance in Doyle's suite.

Neither Doyle nor Ernst could fathom this mystery. They might have been less startled had they seen Houdini's friend Max Berol perform in vaudeville. For many years, in both Europe and America, the ball Berol dipped in ink had spelled out the words called out earlier by members of the audience by rolling across an isolated board. Berol did this by switching a solid cork ball for one with an iron core. A magnet at the end of a rod, manipulated by an assistant concealed behind the board, caused the ball to adhere and move—apparently under its own power. After Berol retired, Houdini purchased the equipment. An assistant in the room adjacent to Houdini's library had opened a small panel in the wall and extended the rod with a magnet through it. The ball on the slate had an iron center, of course.

Ernst had not remembered that when Doyle returned to the room, after writing the words outdoors, Houdini had checked to make sure the slip of paper on which Doyle wrote was folded, then immediately returned it to his friend. Before doing so, the magician had switched slips. While Doyle was busy retrieving the ball from the inkwell and taking it to the board, Houdini read the words. His conversation cued his hidden assistant. Once the message had been written on the slate, Houdini asked Doyle for the folded slip to verify his words. He opened the blank paper, pretended to read from it,

Powell, the magician who headed one of Houdini's *Man From Beyond* stage units. Powell's name came to Houdini's mind at the Atlantic City séance.

then switched it for the original as he returned the paper to his friend. Later, Houdini explained this switching process during his public lectures on fraudulent mediums.

"I did it [the trick] by perfectly normal means," Houdini told Doyle. "I devised it to show you what can be done along these lines. Be careful in future, in endorsing phenomena because you can not explain them."

That June, Sir Arthur, recuperating from the rigors of his cross-country tour, invited the Houdinis to Atlantic City. Harry and Bess checked in at the Ambassador Hotel, where the Doyles were staying.

The first crisis in the relationship between the believer and the doubter occurred on June seventeenth. Lady Doyle had been getting spirit messages by automatic writing. Houdini had still failed to receive a meaningful communication from the mother he adored. Lady Doyle thought it was time she tried for a contact. Seating herself at a table, she held a pencil in her fingers over a blank pad of paper, as her husband prayed. Soon she began writing. She drew a cross at the top of the first page, then filled it and many more with large, hastily scrawled words.

"Oh, my darling, thank God, thank God, at last I'm through. I've tried so often— Now I am happy. Why, of course, I want to talk to my boy—my own beloved boy." Houdini's mother said she loved him, and was preparing a home for him in the afterlife. It was she who had arranged for her son and

Sir Arthur to be brought together: "Tell him to try and write in his own home."

Houdini felt uncomfortable. It seemed odd his Jewish mother should put a Christian cross at the top of the first page. She had always written to him in German. She could not read, write, or speak English. The seventeenth of June was her birthday, but she hadn't mentioned the fact. He wondered about the advice for him "to try and write in his own home."

He asked Lady Doyle what this meant. She said he should sit, as she had done, holding a pencil over a piece of paper, clear his mind of all conscious thought, and his hand would presently begin to write. He picked up a pencil, rested his hand over a sheet of paper, and wrote down the name Powell.

Sir Arthur was thunderstruck. A close friend, Ellis Powell, a medium, had recently died. Doyle suspected Houdini had psychic powers; now he had positive proof of the magician's "secret."

Houdini did not share this opinion. As he explained, Frederick Eugene Powell, an illusionist, had been much in his thoughts during the weekend. Houdini had been negotiating with Powell for him to head one of the stage units to be sent out with the film *The Man from Beyond*. Powell's wife had been sick; he was considering hiring an attractive young woman to take her place in the show.

Doyle refused to accept Houdini's explanation of why he had written the name Powell. Houdini did not believe his mother had communicated with him through Lady Doyle's hand. Each man was too considerate of the other's feelings to express his views forcibly. For the first time they hesitated to speak frankly.

The Doyles were Houdini's guests when he and his wife celebrated their wedding anniversary with a theatre party. The magician sent them a bon-voyage telegram when they sailed for England aboard the *Adriatic*. That October Houdini wrote an article for the *New York Sun*, "Spirit Compacts Unfulfilled." In it he said, "I have never seen or heard anything that could convince me there is a possibility of communication with the loved ones who have gone beyond."

Spiritualism had been a front-page topic while Doyle lectured in the United States. Houdini had avoided a public clash with his friend. Now he girded himself for a crusade—against charlatans who were reaping profit from the Doyle publicity.

In August 1922, Houdini appeared in person with *The Man from Beyond* in Washington, explaining the tricks of dark-room deceptionists, and he wrote a daily column for the *Washington Times*, answering readers' questions about psychic racketeers. When *Scientific American* announced two awards—

"Spirit" photograph made by Alexander Martin, whose talent Sir Arthur Conan Doyle praised.

"Spirit" photograph made by Houdini in New York. Houdini admitted he used trickery.

Another Houdini "spirit" photograph, demonstrating that he too could take out-of-door shots a la the psychics.

"$2,500 for an authentic spirit photograph made under strict test conditions and $2,500 for the first physical manifestations of a psychic nature produced under scientific control"—Houdini became a member of the investigating committee. His associates were Dr. William McDougall, professor of psychology at Harvard and former president of both the British and American societies for psychical research; Dr. Daniel F. Comstock, former member of the Massachusetts Institute of Technology physics department; Dr. Walter Franklin Prince, research officer for the American Society for Psychical Research, and Hereward Carrington, prolific writer on paranormal phenomena, and experienced investigator.

While performing in Los Angeles in April 1923, Houdini acquired an unusual photograph that had been taken the previous month in the First Spiritualist Temple. Mary Fairfield McVickers, a seventy-three-year-old medium, had predicted she would be seen in spirit form if a picture were taken there at 5 P.M. on the day of her funeral. To some, it seemed that ghostly faces were on the print. Houdini went to the building with a photographer and discovered the shadowy images were irregularities in the wall, visible when he stood some distance from it. The photographer took several photographs on plates the magician had purchased; Houdini loaded them in the camera himself. A mysterious streak of light was found on one of the plates when it was developed. Houdini sent copies of this, and the earlier "faces on the wall" photograph to Doyle, then in New York for the start of his second lecture tour. Doyle agreed the irregular wall was responsible for the ghostly faces illusion. He also suggested a scratch on the plate might have caused the "streak of light."

The Houdinis and the Doyles saw each other again in Denver in May. Mrs. Houdini attended Sir Arthur's lecture; the Doyles came to see the magician's show. One of the two or three best spirit photographers in the world lived a short distance away, Doyle said. Houdini arranged for Alexander Martin to take a picture of himself and his assistant, Collins. Four ghostly heads appeared on the photograph—two bewhiskered men, a shrouded woman, and an Indian. Houdini returned for another sitting. This time five ethereal faces turned up on a print—four men with beards; one with a moustache. Three of the men wore glasses. Houdini recognized one face—the man with the moustache was the late Theodore Roosevelt.

Houdini thought Martin used a simple double-exposure technique. Later in New York, he made his own spirit photographs. In one he knelt with his arms around his own astral body; in another he appeared with Abraham Lincoln.

The *Denver Express* of May 9, 1923 ran a startling story headed:

Annie Benninghofen, the reformed medium, appeared with Houdini in Chicago. She explained how she produced "spirit" voices from "floating" trumpets.

Nino Pecoraro, one of the applicants for *Scientific American*'s award, and his nemesis. When Houdini tied him, his powers evaporated.

DOYLE IN DENVER DEFIES HOUDINI

AND OFFERS

TO BRING DEAD BACK AGAIN

Doyle was quoted as saying, "Houdini and I have discussed spiritism before, I have invited him to attend a sitting with me, each of us backing our beliefs with $5,000. I have even offered to bring my dead mother before him in physical form and to talk to her. But we have never got together on it."

Sir Arthur apologetically told Houdini that the reporter had put words in his mouth that he had not uttered; Houdini replied he, too, had frequently been misquoted.

However, the publication in 1924 of Houdini's book, *A Magician Among the Spirits*, brought an end to amicable relations between the doubter and the believer. In his chapter on Sir Arthur Conan Doyle, the magician wrote he treasured his friendship with the distinguished author, who had "a great mind" except where psychic phenomena were concerned. Houdini said he respected Doyle's beliefs and knew he was sincere, but that many of the mediums he championed were frauds, although Sir Arthur refused to accept the fact.

Houdini told of Lady Doyle's séance at Atlantic City, and explained why he was sure the words she had written had not come from his beloved mother.

Doyle had been fascinated by Houdini the man, but after the magician attacked his religious beliefs and held him up to public ridicule, he never wrote or spoke to him again.

Five mediums applied for *Scientific American*'s award for psychical phenomena. Elizabeth Allen Tomson refused to produce her materializations of the dead under rigid control. George Valiantine had not known his chair was wired; the indicator showed he was not in the chair when a trumpet floated at a distance in the dark. The Reverend Josie K. Stewart produced handwritten messages in lavender ink on cards that had been blank by switching prepared cards for the blanks. Nino Pecoraro, bound to a chair by Hereward Carrington, had impressed Sir Arthur Conan Doyle by making a handbell ring, a tambourine spin in the air, and a child's toy piano play. When Houdini tied Pecoraro with several short pieces of rope, there were no manifestations.

The medium known to the public as Margery was by far the strongest contender. Mina Crandon, the blonde, personable, much younger wife of a wealthy Boston surgeon, had discovered her psychic talent in the spring of 1923. To please her husband, she sat with him and some friends around a table in the dark. The table tilted and banged back to the floor. Her psychical progress was rapid. Soon the voice of her dead brother, Walter Stinson, spoke through her vocal cords. A piano stool seemingly under its own volition moved down a corridor; a pigeon appeared from nowhere.

Spirit raps answered her friends' questions. The table rose and floated in the dark. If her husband read of a fantastic feat performed by another medium, Margery found she was able to reproduce it. No two of her séances were ever exactly the same.

Before Dr. Crandon entered his wife in the *Scientific American* competition, he took her abroad. Nobel-prize winner Charles Richet and Gustave Geley, director of a psychic research center in Paris, responded enthusiastically when Margery caused a table to tilt and rise. They marveled as the open-fronted cabinet in which she sat collapsed. In London, Margery gave séances for members of the British College of Psychic Science and the Society for Psychical Research. During a private sitting at the home of Sir Arthur Conan Doyle, a dried flower resting on the mantelpiece flew, apparently unaided, across the room in the dark, landing near Lady Doyle's feet.

On their return to Boston, the Crandons held forty-six séances for invited guests. Then the surgeon told J. Malcolm Bird, an associate editor of the magazine and secretary to the investigating committee, that his wife would compete for the *Scientific American* award. Bird, though not a voting member of the committee, attended fifty-one séances between November 1923 and late December 1924 of the following year—at the doctor's expense. It was Bird who called Mina Crandon the name Margery in his articles to hide her identity. Bird believed she would win the award—then in July 1924 Houdini came to Boston.

The magician knew that either Dr. Crandon or a close friend always sat at the medium's right. Houdini prepared for the possibility he might be invited to sit at her left in a way he kept secret until later.

The circle that night was made up of Margery; R. W. Conant, who worked in committeeman Comstock's laboratory; Orson Munn, the publisher of *Scientific American*; Dr. Crandon; and Houdini the magician. The doctor occupied his usual place at his wife's right; Houdini sat in the chair to her left. Her husband held one of Margery's hands; Houdini took the other. Her right leg pressed against her husband's left one; her left touched Houdini's right. Bird, outside the circle, placed his hand over the linked hands of the Crandons.

The lights were extinguished. The voice of Walter was heard; he whistled and talked. He said a bell box (a battery and an electric bell that rang when the open flap at the top of the box was pushed down to complete a circuit) should be placed on the floor between the magician's feet. The bell rang in the dark while it was there. Walter reported that a megaphone, another of the medium's props, was floating around the room. He asked in which direction the megaphone should be hurled. "Toward me," Houdini responded. It landed with a crash. Later the open-front cabinet in which Margery sat toppled over in the dark.

Houdini and Munn discussed the séance with Bird as he drove them to their hotel. Bird—as usual—was staying with the Crandons.

The ringing of the bell in the box puzzled Bird. Houdini said he had discovered how it was done. That morning he had put a tight elastic bandage on his right leg below the knee. He had removed it shortly before he went to the séance. He knew from experience this would make his skin very sensitive. He had pulled up his trouser leg in the dark. If Margery's leg touched his sensitized skin, he would be able to detect its slightest movement. Slowly she inched her foot toward the bell box until she reached it and pressed down on the top.

The only manifestation that puzzled him was the megaphone tossing. Bird said another committee member had suggested it might have been balanced on Margery's shoulder. No, Houdini decided after some thought, the

Margery (Mina Crandon), Boston medium who applied for *Scientific American*'s prize but did not receive it.

This and the adjacent sketch explain one of the methods Margery used to ring a bell in a box at her séances, according to Houdini.

By tilting her chair, she caused a rung to force down the lid of the bell box, closing the circuit and making the bell sound.

How a Tricky Young Lady Trapped Stupid "Scientists"

"Margery" the spirit-fakir, is a vivacious young lady, happily wedded to a man with a title and a large bank account. She is the wife of Dr. Crandon, a former Professor at the Harvard Medical School. Her pretense of being a "witch", therefore, is not the result of any pecuniary motive.

But she is the victim of a hysterical impulse to pose as a very extraordinary person, possessing some strange supernormal power unknown to modern science. As a means to that end, she devised a crude, amateurish, silly performance, given in total darkness, and pretended that it was proof that the dead return at her bidding. But only half-witted persons would think of taking such a farce seriously.

Now "The Scientific American" had offered a prize of $2,500 for genuine ghost phenomena, and incredible though it may seem, Margery had the nerve to apply for the job.

Hereward Carrington, the famous cigarette smoker, whose wild spiritistic trash has had so much prominence in the newspapers and magazines as "scientific research", and who spends most of his time groping about in the Spiritistic Sewer, looking for something that can be commercialized, and Birdy Malcom, the celebrated authority on pre-historic fly-specks, made a protracted and "scientific" study of "Margery" and concluded that the young lady was too nice to cheat, and that she should be given the cash. Why did they do such a thing? Here is the answer:

To facilitate the investigation, Margery gave them a cordial invitation to spend their summer vacations at her spacious and well furnished home, where she entertained them sumptuously. She gave them three bounteous meals a day, and downy beds to sleep on at night, after the ice cream and hooch had run out, and all at her own expense. Wasn't that nice?

We can easily see Hereward and Birdy, with napkins stuck into their collars, pushing custard pie into their faces with their knives, and wondering how they managed to strike such easy graft. Is it any wonder that they decided in favor of the lady? How could they brand their charming hostess a liar and fraud after she had wined and dined them for so long a time?

Hereward's meal ticket isn't quite so certain as Birdy's and if it were not for occasional handouts, he would have to accept a position behind Macey's ribbon counter.

As Eve tempted Adam, so did the bewitching Margery tempt the peanut-head "scientists". She intimated that if she raked off the $2,500 she would donate it to some worthy investigation of "psychic phenomena". And who but these "experts" could be considered worthy of Margery's gift? Surely this was enough to bias the mind of any "scientific" authority on ghosts:

When The Scientific American discovered that Carrington and Bird were making fools of themselves, it expunged the advertised Margery report.

Spiritism is a Superstition. Don't be Deceived by Deluded Propagandists.

Leaflet prepared by Houdini or Oscar S. Teale, a member of his staff.

megaphone had been on her head like a dunce cap. With a snap of her head, she could send it in any direction. Several times during the sitting, the séance had been interrupted. The lights had been turned on, then switched off again. Directly after one of these intermissions, Houdini explained, Margery could have quickly picked up the megaphone from the floor, put it on her head with her right hand, then tilted the lightweight cabinet back just enough to slide her right foot under the nearest panel. There was always some delay while hands were being grasped to re-form the circle. She would then be ready to send the "floating" megaphone toward any sitter and to upset the cabinet with a swift kick.

At Houdini's second séance with Margery the following night, he again was aware when she extended her foot toward the bell box, and he learned how Margery performed another of her tricks. When a table tipped on two legs in the dark he released his grip on Munn's hand, felt under the table, and found Margery's head.

She had leaned forward to get in this position. When she raised her head, she lifted the table. He later discovered a fast upward movement was sufficient to overturn the table.

Houdini returned to Boston in August with a contraption designed to prevent Margery from using her hands and her feet to produce fraudulent phenomena. This was a wooden box similar to a crate for an old-fashioned slant-top desk. It was large enough to hold the medium seated comfortably on a chair inside it. Semicircular sections had been cut from the hinged front and top portions. When these were closed around the medium's neck, only her head protruded. At the sides were holes through which she could extend her hands. Extra strips of wood could be nailed over these openings should the committee decide to have her hands confined within the box.

When Dr. Crandon saw this container, he objected so violently that the investigators agreed to let Margery first get used to the box by giving a familiarization séance for her friends behind closed doors. After it was over, her supporters left the room, and the *Scientific American* group filed in. This séance ended abruptly when the hinged front portion of the box clattered down in the dark. Dr. Crandon said Walter must have forced the box open. Houdini claimed Margery had used her shoulders to dislodge the narrow brass strips that held the panels closed. He had not challenged the medium to escape from the box; its purpose was to prevent trickery.

The committee left the room; Margery's friends returned for another practice session behind closed doors. When the committee came back, Walter sarcastically asked Houdini how much he was being paid to stop the manifestations. No further phenomena were produced. Eventually Walter told a committee member to examine the bell box in the light. A small round eraser, the sort usually found on the end of a lead pencil, was wedged under the flap. Four times the usual amount of pressure would be required to depress the flap and ring the bell. Houdini immediately made a statement for the record that he had not put the eraser there.

The magician reinforced the fraud-prevention box, adding heavy hasps, staples, and four padlocks. On the evening of August 26, Houdini held Margery's left hand, which extended from his side of the box; Dr. Walter Franklin Prince took her right hand on the far side. This was an important procedural change. Up till now, the medium's husband had been the "control" on her right. Houdini warned his fellow committeeman he must not even for a moment release the medium's hand. When Margery asked him why he made such an issue of this, Houdini replied that as long as her hands were outside the box, she would be unable to take hold of any object she might previously have smuggled within.

Soon Walter spoke up and implied Houdini had put a ruler under the cushion on which the medium's feet were resting. He became abusive: "Houdini, you goddamned son of a bitch, get the hell out of here and never come back. If you don't, I will."

When the box was unlocked, a new carpenter's ruler, a two-foot length folded in four six-inch sections, was found beneath the pillow. It was suggested that Collins, Houdini's assistant, might have left the ruler there when he strengthened the box. But when Collins was summoned for questioning, he said his ruler was still in his pocket. He pulled it out and displayed it.

Houdini then dictated a statement: "I wish it recorded that I demanded Collins to take a sacred oath on the life of his mother that he did not put the ruler into the box and knew positively nothing about it. I also pledge my sacred word of honor as a man that the first I knew of the ruler in the box was when I was so informed by Walter."

In *Houdini Exposes the Tricks Used by the Boston Medium "Margery"*, the magician said that during the third and last of the committee séances held in 1924, Dr. Crandon commented, "Some day, Houdini, you will see the light, and if it were to occur this evening, I would gladly give ten thousand dollars to charity."

"It may happen, but I doubt it," Houdini answered.

"Yes, sir," the surgeon repeated, "if you were converted this evening I would willingly give ten thousand dollars to charity."

That night Margery's legs and feet were immobilized by a device constructed by committeeman Comstock. With the bell box on the floor and her hands held by someone other than her husband, there were no phenomena.

The final *Scientific American* committee report on Margery was released in February 1925. Carrington, who had lived at the Crandon house during his investigations, said the medium had produced some genuine phenomena. Comstock said he had never witnessed a manifestation under strict scientific control. McDougall, the first member of the committee to attend one of Margery's séances and the last to send in his opinion, had seen nothing that would lead him to believe means other than normal had been employed. He thought the Crandons were testing the gullibility of scientists. Houdini called the medium a fraud. By a 4 to 1 vote, Margery did not receive the *Scientific American* award.

Dr. Crandon had mailed Sir Arthur Conan Doyle stenographic accounts of Margery's séances. Sir Arthur believed Mrs. Crandon to be a genuine psychic. But then he also thought that Houdini was a medium. He wrote Harold Kellock, a Houdini biographer, on September 19, 1929: "I have no more doubt that he used psychic power than I have that I am dictating this letter." In *The Edge of the Unknown*, his last book, Sir Arthur wrote that Houdini was "the most curious and intriguing" person he ever met. He predicted the mystifier would "live in history with such personalities as Cagliostro, the Chevalier D'Eon, and other strange characters."

Neither Houdini nor Doyle was alive in 1932 when E. E. Dudley, a believer, announced a sensational discovery. For many years he had endeavored to prove that spirit fingerprints frequently produced by Margery on hot wax in the dark had been made, as both the medium and Walter claimed, by her dead brother. Alas, Dudley found that the prints were indisputably those of a living man—Margery's dentist!

DRESDENER KUNDSCHAU, DRESDEN, SAXONY

The stories Houdini devised for this publication were indeed
weird. Some were fascinating, but not one was true.

6

Houdini the Magician

Houdini's crusade against fraudulent mediums was acclaimed by prominent clergymen and the press; his films had also enhanced his fame as an escapologist; and for eight years he had been president of both the Society of American Magicians and the Magicians Club of London, yet in 1925 when he celebrated his fifty-first birthday, he had yet to fulfill his greatest ambition. Houdini had never toured with his own full-length show in the tradition of Robert-Houdin, Herrmann the Great, and Harry Kellar.

He had always wanted to present illusions, to play in legitimate theatres with a production that would appeal to sophisticated audiences. However, once he had established himself as a daredevil escapologist, he could never convince bookers that his magic would appeal to the public as much as his dramatic self-releases.

Too poor as a young man to buy evening clothes or expensive apparatus, Houdini had performed in a costume made by his mother. His act depended principally on his skill at sleight of hand and his personality.

Once he earned sufficient money, he bought a dress suit and invested in

Kellar gave his farewell
performance in Baltimore on
May 16, 1908, at Ford's Theatre.

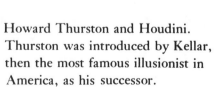

Howard Thurston and Houdini.
Thurston was introduced by **Kellar**,
then the most famous illusionist in
America, as his successor.

publicity material. His first half-sheet lithographed poster proclaimed him the "King of Cards." Illustrations above and below his portrait depicted him adroitly flipping over a ribbon of cards spread precariously along his outstretched arm and executing intricate triple cuts as he held a deck with one hand.

His single sizable feat was Metamorphosis, the quick transposition between Houdini, locked in a trunk, and his brother Theo, behind the drapes of a cabinet. This continued to be the closing number long after Houdini's wife took his brother's place and Houdini became a headliner.

While Houdini struggled to maintain his reputation as a challenge escape star, T. Nelson Downs, an expert coin manipulator from Iowa, held audiences enrapt with minimal exertion. The two were friendly rivals.

"Travelers from Europe report the existence of a powerful mutual-admiration society composed entirely of magicians whose acts are features," *Mahatma*, the American magic monthly, noted in July 1901. The passwords, it reported, were "Houdini, I've seen all kinds of magic acts, but without any exception, yours is really the acme of perfection" and "Downs, I don't often praise a man, but whenever I see your act I can't help thinking that there can never be another act conceived that will be so really marvelous." *Mahatma* thus hinted there were only two members in this society.

Houdini, then headlining in Cologne, mailed a reply to the editor.

I note you have exposed the password of the powerful M.A.A. which is composed of all magicians who are not jealous of each other. . . . It is a Mutual Admiration Association, and as you have either willfully exposed or unknowingly published the passwords, I would ask you to kindly send me the name of the member who delivered the secrets to you. . . . Who was it? The fine for telling secrets of the M.A.A. is to pay the bus fare of the other member's journey for life, thus you can see our laws are very stringent. . . . As this is the first organization of its kind that has ever been formed, its career is being carefully watched and studied. . . .

> Respectfully yours,
> HANDCUFF HOUDINI
> Vice-President of the M.A.A.

P.S. T. Nelson Downs is at the present writing the president of the M.A.A. He is the best president the association has ever had.

This two-man club predated what is now the oldest organization of conjurers in the world; the Society of American Magicians was founded the following year.

Proud of his digital dexterity, Houdini could not resist exhibiting his manual skill during his first Paris engagement. Rolling up his sleeves, he displayed his right hand back and front, then one by one produced thirty-two playing cards from his fingertips. French magicians applauded this more than they had his dramatic releases from manacles.

Houdini's private performances invariably included more magic than escapology. In 1903 at Kleinmichel Palace in Moscow he amazed for ninety minutes Grand Duke Sergius and other members of the Russian nobility. A second-sight routine that Houdini had perfected with his wife while traveling with the Welsh Brothers Circus in the United States received prolonged applause. In this routine, Houdini cued Bess in various ways. For instance, he trained one ear to wiggle. When he stood in profile at the front of the stage, she alone could see the twitches that signaled numbers or letters of the alphabet. Conveying the fifteenth letter of the alphabet, his ear would wiggle once, stand still, then five additional movements would indicate that the letter was O.

When Bess was blindfolded, Houdini's seemingly casual conversation secretly transmitted further information. Intrigued by this mystery, the Grand Duchess took Houdini aside and begged him to teach her the routine. Later that evening, after they had practiced, she announced to her friends that she, too, had telepathic gifts. Houdini tied a handkerchief over her eyes. He touched several objects in the room; gleefully, she identified them.

As a memento of the occasion, Sergius presented to the magician a jeweled champagne ladle. When this was put on display in the living room of Houdini's house in New York City, he often told guests how he had acquired it, stressing that no other mystifier had ever had a Russian grand duchess as assistant.

As always, later writers embroidered upon Houdini's feats. One story is that he astonished Muscovites by causing the bells of the Kremlin to peal at his command. The imaginative writer who made up this story also proposed a method for performing the trick; the magician, he said, created the illusion by having an unseen rifleman stand at the window of a nearby building and fire at the bell tower.

Preparing for the time when he would take his own magic show on the road, Houdini accumulated apparatus in Europe—replicas of devices made by Robert-Houdin; the complete vaudeville act of Hermalin, a British conjurer; and various unusual illusions. Then, in the spring of 1914, "the World Famous Self Liberator" made his debut as "the Supreme Ruler of Mystery." Other conjurers had billed themselves as "the Napoleon of Necromancy" and "the Eighth Wonder of the World." Houdini sought to outdo them, promising on his posters that he "would prove himself to be the Greatest Mystifier that History Chronicles."

T. Nelson Downs, the best of coin conjurers, and Houdini frequently played on the same vaudeville bills in Europe. They had worked together in the United States before Downs sailed for London.

Each admired the other's skill, so they formed a two-man Mutual Admiration Association.

When they met years later, Houdini stood on his toes as a photographer took a picture, not realizing that a full-length shot had been made.

He arranged to break in the new act in the British provinces. Theatre owners, eager to book the most-publicized variety entertainer in England, agreed to let Houdini try out his magic routine several times during the week if he would present his sensational Water Torture Cell at the other performances.

The Grand Magical Revue began with Houdini passing coins invisibly across the stage and into a small, closed "crystal casket," suspended by ribbons from above. Good-bye Winter was described in his advertisements as "Vanishing a live, breathing human being in mid-air, away from all curtains and in full glare of lights in less than ONE MILLIONTH OF A SECOND." A young woman in furs stood on the uppermost of two stacked tables. Houdini, climbing a ladder, draped a cloth over her, covering her from head to toe. He then descended the ladder, reached up, and whipped away the cover: She was gone!

Money from Nothing was Houdini's version of the Miser's Dream. He walked down the aisles producing "£1,000 in genuine Gold and Silver . . . in a manner never shown before by any performer past and present."

The Arrival of Summer, described as "Materializing in a most inexplicable manner a FAIRY QUEEN GARDENER under strictest conditions possible . . . deceiving the Five Senses in one fell swoop," involved an odd-shaped box, in which angular doors were opened to prove that the box was empty. Abracadabra! a garlanded girl then stepped out from the interior.

After "Calico Conjuring. An Object Lesson for the Ladies" came the closing illusion: "two human beings transported through space and walls of steel-bound oaken boards, outstripping the rapidity of thought, after being bound, gagged and sealed by a committee selected from the audience."

Houdini's opening trick, the Crystal Casket, linked him with the man who had been his idol; the replica of Robert-Houdin's glass box had been made in Paris. His last illusion, his old reliable Metamorphosis trunk mystery, always insured several bows.

The show reached King's Hall, Dover, the week of June 1, 1914. Press releases said this was Houdini's "last week but one in Great Britain"; on June eighteenth he planned to sail on the *Imperator* for "a tour around the world."

The most fascinating addition to the Grand Magical Revue had been invented by Buatier de Kolta, an ingenious French illusionist who died in 1903, in New Orleans, Louisiana. Leah Goldston, the wife of Will Goldston, a London magic dealer, had subsequently acquired the original equipment; she, in turn, sold it to Houdini.

Removing an eight-inch die from a satchel, Houdini placed the cube on a low platform, raised from the stage on four short legs. At his command,

Advertisement for Houdini's illusion act in England. In 1914, he had planned to tour with this in the United States, then travel around the world. His notations indicate his enthusiasm for the project.

Hamburg-Amerika Linie

CONCERT-ENTERTAINMENT

for the benefit of the

German Sailors Home and the Magicians Club in London, England.

---

1. The Ritz Carlton Orchestra

Kapellmeister A. Sonnenschein

From the Op. "La Bohéme .... Puccini

2. Madame A. Cortesao

Dramatic Soprano

From the Op. "Madame Butterfly"............. Puccini

3. Mr. Harry Houdini

The world famous Self Liberator and Mystifier in his various acts

First Part

a. Jessie James feat of defeating the gallows

b. The camelion handkerchiefs

c. A lesson in magic

d. Wine and water

e. Card sleights extraordinary

f. The power of mind over matter

g. Egyptian Priests burnt turban

h. Arabian night, Persian egg bag trick

i. Spiritulistic Slate test in full glare of the light

k. East Indian needle trick

Ritz Carlton Orchestra

Der Rosenkavalier .... Strauß

Second Part

Houdini will demonstrate his skill in escaping
from any Regulation Handcuff or Leg-Iron

l. Exposing his method of escaping from the German Transport Chain

m. Showing the release from the French Thumb-screw

The Bean-giant

n. By escaping from this cuff Houdini won $ 500 from the inventor and thereby laid the foundation of his Reputation

o. Seamen will lock Houdini up in the Imperator Irons

Shipboard show program. Theodore Roosevelt was amazed by the slate test.

the die instantly expanded many times in size. Houdini then removed the hollow three-foot-square cube to reveal a young woman, seated cross-legged, on the platform.

Delighted by the response to his conjuring in Dover, Houdini wrote on the margin of a playbill, "Said by all the great English critics to be the Best Mystery Show ever Presented. An almost original programme." Bookers who had journeyed to size up the attraction in Dover and in Nottingham disagreed. Houdini the escapologist was worth every penny big city theatres would pay him; Houdini the magician was only one of many capable illusionists.

Shortly before embarking on the *Imperator* en route to New York, Houdini learned that Theodore Roosevelt, the former President of the United States, would be on the same ship. Roosevelt had led an expedition to a remote uncharted area of South America. A London reporter gave Houdini a copy of a map that had not yet been printed and details of the journey.

Houdini hoped to utilize this material when he performed at the ship's concert. If he could subtly lead Roosevelt to think of an appropriate question, an extraordinary feat was possible. No matter what happened, the magician would later have an anecdote to tell about an American he admired.

After several preliminary tricks, Houdini invited several members of the audience to picture in their minds exotic areas they had seen in the past year and then to write a question about the places. Roosevelt received one of the slips of paper distributed by Houdini. Before he could even begin to write, Victor Herbert, the famous composer, leaning over from an adjoining chair, suggested that Roosevelt should turn his back so that the magician would be unable to observe the movements of his pencil. Roosevelt followed this advice, then folded the paper. Houdini took it, and as he talked, secretly opened the slip and read the words. Deftly refolding the paper, the magician returned it, then picked up two blank slates from his table. After displaying them, he placed one atop the other; then parting them like the facing pages of a book, he instructed Roosevelt to drop his question between the two. Houdini then tied the slates together. Stressing that he had no supernormal powers, he assumed the role of a medium, calling on "the spirits" to answer the question.

Roosevelt had asked, "Where was I last Christmas?" When the slates were untied, a chalked map with an arrow pointing to the River of Doubt appeared on one; the other carried the words, "Near the Andes," with the signature of W. T. Stead, a British journalist-spiritualist who had perished two years earlier when the *Titanic* sank. Roosevelt was properly flabbergasted.

An account of this startling feat was sent by the *Imperator*'s radio operator to Newfoundland. From there, a relay station beamed it to New York. The story appeared in print before the ship docked.

When Roosevelt posed for a picture with six fellow passengers one sunny afternoon, Houdini stood by his side. The magician made copies of this photograph after having had the original retouched, so that only he and the *Imperator*'s most distinguished traveler could be seen.

Houdini's opening performance in July 1914 at Hammerstein's Roof Garden in New York City featured the Water Torture Cell. At the beginning of his second week, the magician introduced Walking Through a Brick Wall.

Twice daily, bricklayers built a nine-foot-high wall in a steel frame on a wheeled base. After the mortar had dried, a committee of thirty members of the audience inspected the wall and two threefold screens of canvas. Houdini's assistants then unrolled a rug on the stage; over this a large muslin cloth was spread. His assistants positioned the wall in the center of the muslin, with one end of the structure facing toward the footlights. Solid brick could be seen by those on the stage to the left, to the right, and above the screen. The thirty committeemen stood at the sides and back of the stage, leaving a clear space in front for the audience to have an unobstructed view.

Wearing a long white coat, Houdini walked to the wall. When he reached it, one of the six-foot-high, three-panel screens was moved to enclose him. The other screen was placed directly opposite on the other side of the wall. For a moment Houdini extended his hands over the top of the screen, shouting, "Here I am; now I'm gone!" His assistants speedily opened the screen's panels. Houdini had indeed vanished. They ran to the opposite side of the wall and pulled away the second screen. Houdini, smiling enigmatically, stepped forward.

He had purchased the secret of this illusion in England in May from Sydney Joselyne. Joselyne said it was his invention, though he had specified the penetration of a wall of steel rather than brick. The following month, P. T. Selbit, an outstanding creator of illusions, presented Walking Through a Brick Wall at Maskelyne and Devant's St. George's Hall in London—and claimed that *he* had originated the feat. In Selbit's case, the wall was built before the performance, and members of the audience were invited to strike it with hammers to prove its solidity. Selbit did not go through the wall himself; an attractive young woman, wearing a long dress and a wide-brimmed hat, passed mysteriously from one side to the other. A comparison of drawings of the metal frameworks used to support Houdini's and Selbit's walls indicates they were identical.

Above: Retouched photograph of Houdini
and Theodore Roosevelt on the *Imperator*.
Other passengers in the picture were elimi-
nated. *At left:* The original shipboard picture,
before alteration for reproduction.

After producing hundreds of yards of
silk from a bowl of water at the
New York Hippodrome in 1918,
Houdini conjured up an American eagle.
Wartime audiences gave him an ovation.

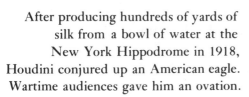

Houdini featured the illusion for three weeks at Hammerstein's, then, having reaped the maximum publicity, gave it to his brother. Theatre bookers were not interested in this or the other illusions Houdini imported from Europe; they signed him to tour with the Water Torture Cell. There was only one consolation. He would do the East Indian Needle Trick as a prelude.

Four years passed before the frustrated illusionist had another opportunity to intrigue theatre audiences with a big-scale marvel. Charles Morritt, the British inventor of The Disappearing Donkey, informed Houdini he had worked out a way to make an elephant disappear. Intrigued by the idea, Houdini purchased the worldwide performing rights. There were technical difficulties. Morritt's donkey had been trained to operate the device that brought about the disappearance. Houdini knew a man would have to be in the cabinet with the elephant to perform this function. Then there was the problem of finding an elephant.

Houdini discussed the illusion with Charles Dillingham, producer of the spectacular New York Hippodrome revues. The Hippodrome had 5,697 seats; how appropriate to feature the largest illusion ever devised on that mammoth stage! The elephant? Dillingham would book Powers' Elephants, a popular animal act, on the bill. Houdini could take his choice of five.

Houdini's Vanishing Elephant disappeared for the first time on January 7, 1918. The program heralded:

"The Most Colossal Disappearing Mystery that History Records. Dissolving into thin air, on the largest stage in the world, an elephant weighing 10,000 pounds. Before one's very eyes in a full blaze of light with bewildering rapidity, this pachyderm monster suddenly eludes the vision."

The curtains opened on a bare stage. Houdini introduced Jennie, "the daughter of P. T. Barnum's famous Jumbo." Out from the wings lumbered the elephant, adorned with a bright blue ribbon, tied in a bow around her neck. Strapped to her left hind leg was an alarm clock. Cued by her trainer, Jennie reared up on her hind legs and flourished her trunk. Settling back, she approached the magician and seemed to kiss him on the cheek. (Actually she reached for sugar cubes in his hand.) Twelve stagehands pushed a heavy wooden box, "the size of a small garage," to the center of the stage. A ramp was fitted in place at one side. Jennie, paced by her trainer, circled the box, then went up the ramp with him and walked inside. She wore the "wristwatch," Houdini explained, so spectators could see her until the very last second. The ramp was taken away. Curtains were closed at the entrance, and the box was then hauled around until the curtained entrance faced the

For nineteen weeks—the longest theatre engagement of his career—Houdini featured the Vanishing Elephant at the Hippodrome in New York City.

Newspaper advertisement for the 1918 spectacle on the world's largest stage.

audience. Houdini fired a pistol. The curtains were thrown open, and a large circular section was removed from the back of the box. Spectators could see through the box to the stage curtains far at the rear. The elephant had disappeared!

"Houdini puts his title of premier escape artist behind him and becomes the Master Magician," Sime Silverman, editor of *Variety,* the theatrical weekly, stated in his rave review. He added, "Matinée crowds will worry themselves into sleep nightly wondering what Houdini did with his elephant."

Neither Silverman nor other perceptive critics noted that the trainer had disappeared along with the elephant. During this show, Houdini also released himself from a box submerged in the Hippodrome pool, but for once his magic eclipsed his escapology. The Vanishing Elephant brought him the longest run of his career—nineteen weeks.

Houdini returned to the Hippodrome in August, after completing *The Master Mystery,* a film serial, in Yonkers, New York, again appearing twice on the bill. Though he had fractured three bones in his left wrist during the months of moviemaking, Houdini wriggled free from a straitjacket, suspended head-down over the stage.

His new magic sequence stirred the wartime audiences. Houdini struck a sheet of glass to show it was solid. He put the glass on top of a small table, then set a fishbowl on the glass. To the water already in the transparent bowl, he added red and blue liquids. Mixing the solution until the water turned black, he capped the bowl with a paper drumhead. Baring his right arm to the elbow, he plunged his hand through the paper and into the liquid, whipping out a vast cascade of silk, forty inches wide and four hundred feet long.

As the music built to a crescendo, he dipped his hand into the bowl again and pulled out a ribbon attached to a succession of giant flags—emblems of the Allied nations. Assistants extended the flags from one side of the huge stage to the other. Striding over to the Stars and Stripes, Houdini reached beneath its folds and produced a live, wing-flapping American eagle. Cheering spectators gave him an ovation.

During the next few years, Houdini's attention centered on motion pictures; he made two feature-length films for Jesse Lasky, then *The Man from Beyond,* which he wrote, starred in, and produced himself. For the premiere in April 1922 and during the three-week run at the Times Square Theatre on Broadway, Houdini made personal appearances with a magic show that encompassed everything from the tiny needle-threading trick to the enormous Vanishing Elephant. He conjured away Winter in her furs and materi-

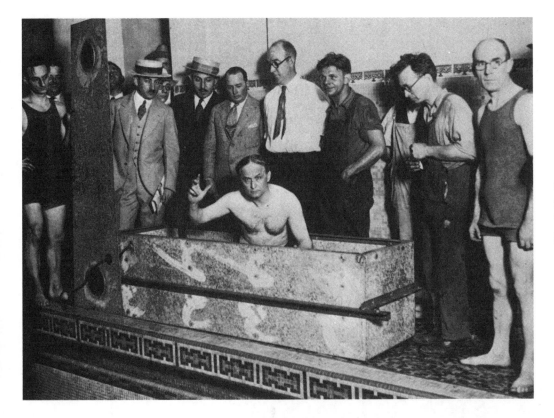

Sealed inside an air-tight box at the Hotel Shelton pool in New York City, Houdini was lowered beneath the water.

Rahmah Bey, a fakir, claimed he survived in a box of precisely the same size for an hour because of his psychic power. Houdini ridiculed this statement, and stayed sealed up thirty minutes longer

HOUDINI

IN PERSON

Without a Peer in the Realm of Magic

will introduce at every performance his Original Creations:

GOOD-BYE WINTER

Disappearing a human being in mid-air and in full
glare of light

ARRIVAL OF SUMMER

A production.   An apparant materialization of a human
being, surrounded by a committee of judges.

THE YOGI MASTERPIECE

The East Indian Needle Mystery

RELEASING HIMSELF FROM A STRAIGHT JACKET

Such as is used on the murderous insane.   In full view
of his audience.

and concluding with

THE GREATEST VANISHMENT THE WORLD HAS EVER KNOWN

The Disappearing Elephant

The instantaneous disappearance of a 10,000 pound elephant

Mothers, Your Boys Love Mystery
Fathers, Here is Your Alibi to Witness the Unusual
The Greatest Mystery Show the World Has Ever Known

TIMES SQUARE THEATRE TWICE DAILY NOW

42nd STREET, NEAR BROADWAY   NEW YORK CITY

Houdini revived his elephant illusion at the Times Square Theatre
in 1922 when he appeared with his film *The Man From Beyond*.

The president of the S.A.M. appeared on the cover of the 1924 banquet menu.

His Christmas cards, in later years, carried a bit of Houdini humor.

alized Spring, adorned with flowers. Knots were tied with a flick of his wrist in silk scarfs, then passed magically from one set of foulards to another. With volunteers on the stage, he exhibited his finesse with cards, and not to disappoint the fans who would see his thrilling escapades in the film, he squirmed and contorted to release himself from a straitjacket.

Houdini's friend Sir Arthur Conan Doyle had aroused widespread interest in Spiritualism as he lectured across the nation.

Houdini set out to enlighten a confused public that was turning to mediums in hopes of reaching departed loved ones but the crowds attending his lectures in concert halls came more to see him perform than to listen to his charges of chicanery. To say a psychic switched slates to produce a message on a blank surface was not enough; he had to show how the exchange was made. Because audiences demanded it, he demonstrated what a skillful conjurer could do without the aid of spirits.

At the New York Hippodrome, where earlier he had whisked away elephants and produced eagles, Houdini now duplicated the feats of alleged psychics. Tied to a chair inside a curtained cabinet, he caused a tambourine to jangle and a hand bell to ring. After an assistant put a sharp knife on the floor near the chair, Houdini—not the spirits—slashed the ropes, then walked forward to accept the applause.

Locked inside the wooden crate he had constructed for Margery, the Boston medium, his head protruding from the neck-sized hole in the top, facing a bell box on a table in front of the crate, Houdini said that rather than turn out the stage lights, his assistants would enshroud the crate and the table with a large black cloth. Houdini's head stayed in view, extending up through a hole in the center of the cloth. It seemed impossible for him to make the bell box on the table sound, but ring it did—starting and stopping at his whim.

Later, as two volunteers (they were hooded, to simulate the darkness of a séance) held his hands and controlled his feet with their feet, Houdini announced that a megaphone would rise, float, then crash down as one had done at a séance given by Margery. Houdini told the man on his right to make sure the megaphone was still on the floor. The hooded volunteer released his grip on the magician's hand to grope for the megaphone. As soon as he touched it, Houdini quickly picked up the megaphone with his free hand, put it on his head and had his hand back by his side when the spectator reached for it. He asked the volunteer where the "floating" megaphone should land, then snapped his head and sent the megaphone flying in the specified direction.

During a six-week run at the Hippodrome in 1925, Houdini played the role of "Zanetti," a medium, answering the sealed questions given to him by

Senator Arthur Capper seated with Houdini when he endorsed anti-fortune-telling legislation in Washington in 1924. Neither the bill proposed to a Senate committee nor the one considered by a House committee passed.

members of the audience who substituted for clients, and then, to quote the program, "showing how writing is secured in full light on slates brought by skeptics."

Houdini sat at the left side of a table. A man from the audience took the chair opposite him. The volunteer looked under the draped table and found nothing there except a dinner bell. He placed the tips of his shoes on top of Houdini's shoes, then reaching across the table, gripped Houdini's hands. Houdini asked if spirits were present. The bell under the table rang loudly. When the volunteer posed questions that could be answered by no, maybe, or yes, the bell rang, once, twice, or three times in reply. The volunteer controlled the magician's hands and feet; no one approached the table.

Eventually, an assistant lifted the front portion of the tablecloth while the bell was ringing. Houdini had slipped his right foot from its shoe. His stocking had been cut away at the end. He had grasped the handle of the bell between his big and second toes and was ringing it by shaking his foot. A roar of laughter came from the audience. When the volunteer bent down to see what had provoked this response, he laughed, too.

Houdini had triumphed as an escapologist, a magician, and an exposer of mediumistic fraud. That summer when he planned a full-evening show for the fall, he decided to include all these elements.

In England, in addition to the illusions he featured in his Grand Magical Revue, Houdini had acquired a "Noah's Ark"; water poured into it

Houdini the Magician
163

Shubert Majestic
THEATRE

Messrs. LEE & J. J. SHUBERT, Managing Directors

Telephone Beach 4520   Seats also at Little Bldg. at Box Office Prices

Beginning Monday, September 13, 1926

L. LAWRENCE WEBER

Has the Honor to Offer

Master Mystifier
HOUDINI

Acclaimed by Press and Public

"The Greatest Necromancer of the Age—Perhaps of All Times."
—(Literary Digest)

Who Presents

AN ENTIRE EVENING'S ENTERTAINMENT

Consisting of Many Original Mysteries Never Before Equaled in

the Realm of Magic Art

"THREE SHOWS IN ONE"

Magic, Illusions, Escapes, and Fraud Mediums Exposed

NOTE: During Houdini's performance it will be necessary to invite a committee of investigators on the stage, and the management assures all volunteers that no practical jokes of any kind will be perpetrated on anyone.

Almost every experiment presented by Houdini is his original invention and creation.

PROGRAM SUBJECT TO CHANGE

In the event that challenges are made and accepted, certain features of the program will be deleted to make space for those added.

PLEASE NOTE

A number of illusions and experiments are programmed, but the performance would be too extensive if they were all presented during the evening. Houdini, however, will vary his entertainment by presentations from the following:

PROGRAM
ACT I
Magic

The Crystal Casket
Conradi's Aladdin's Lamp
The Magical Rose Bush
Queen Bess' Bunny
The Arrival and Departure of Ponzi
Izaak Walton Eclipsed
Birds in a Gilded Cage
The Mystical Huntsman
Doves of Peace
The Flying Handkerchief
Intelligent Fingers
Red Magic
The Flight of Time

Fleurette's Transition
Slicing a Woman
The Egyptian Turban
Metamorphosis—The exchange of
   Human Beings in a locked, sealed
   and corded trunk
Money for Nothing
The Slave Girl's Lament
Summertime
Wintertime
Radio of 1950
Ponce De Leon's Dream Realized
A lesson from Ching Ling Foo

The magic routine in Houdini's full-evening show varied from city to city. New mysteries were tested almost every week.

CARD SLEIGHTS: Houdini was the first to present the forward and back palm.

Houdini presents today card manipulations, such as his fifty-two card forward and back palm, which gained for him the title of "King of Cards" more than thirty years ago. Many of his original passes and sleights have been used by most all of the present-day magicians.

The Card Star (Herr Doebler's Masterpiece).

The Miracles of Mahatma.

The Whirlwind of Colors.

Ten Minute Intermission

ACT II

The Famous East Indian Needle Mystery.

The Celebrated Chinese Water Torture Cell. (Nothing like it has ever been attempted by any other magician).

The Secret of the Sphinx.

Ten Minute Intermission

ACT III
The Ribbon Curtain

Special attention is called to the blue curtain, which may appear like a crazy-quilt pattern. Twenty-five years ago, Houdini, touring Continental Europe, broke records in every theatre in which he appeared. It was the custom in those days to present the artist with a huge laurel wreath, a la Marathon winner, and the ribbons are from the following managers and theatre owners: Berlin Winter Garden, Berlin, Germany; Herr Director Kamsetzer, Central Theatre, Dresden, Saxony; Director Bruck, Frankfort on Main; Director Tichy, Prague, Bohemia; Director Tom Barresford, Alhambra Theatre, Paris, France; Director C. Dundas Slater, Alhambra Theatre, London, England; Director Hippodrome, London, England; Director Harry Rickards, Australia; Director Gluck, Dusseldorf; Director L. Lerin, Rembrandt Theatre, Amsterdam, Holland; Director Corty, Althoff; Director Busch, Berlin; Director Carre, Holland; Director M. Wolf, Essen, Ruhr; Director Waldman Roanocher, Vienna; Director Reichshallen, Cologne; Director Mellini, Hanover; Director Hagenbeck, Luttick and Brussels; Director Lorensen, Cophenhagen; Director Bremen, Dorthmund.

DO THE DEAD COME BACK?

A series of natural phenomena puzzling the most intelligent and erudite people of the world. The majority of the problems are frequently attributed to demonology and witchcraft.

That there may be no mistake in Houdini's attitude, he wishes it to be thoroughly and clearly understood that he is not attacking any religion in any way. He is not a skeptic and respects genuine believers. He does not say there is no such thing, but that he has never met a genuine medium. He is simply exposing the fraudulent mediums. At the end of the performance there will be a limited amount of time for what may be called an open forum. In this Houdini is willing to answer any and all rational questions on the subject. He has no desire to spread false propaganda, and if wrong will be delighted to be corrected, but at no time, however, will he discuss the Bible, or Biblical quotations, before the audience.

ZANETTI'S SPIRIT BRIDE

THE SLATE TEST

The secrets of fraudulent medium message reading exposed. One of the most profitable methods.

HOW MEDIUMS CAUSE WILLS TO BE CHANGED

The materialization of baby hands and fingers. How hands and feet are held and the medium manages to have the spirits ring bells and rattle tambourines.

THE OPEN FORUM

Any medium who can prove to a selected committee that he possesses a weird or psychic power can win the following rewards offered in America: $10,000 by Mr. J. F. Rinn, $500 by Dr. J. Allen Gilbert, $5,000 by the *Scientific American*, and Houdini's $10,000. For public record, Houdini is a member of the committee of the *Scientific American*.

HOUDINI'S $10,000 CHALLENGE

Open to any medium in the world (male or female). Houdini will wager the above-mentioned sum, the money to go to charity, if the spiritualists will produce a medium presenting any physical phenomena that he cannot reproduce or explain by natural means.

Condition: The medium must present the manifestation three times, in the presence of Houdini and the selected committee.

NOTE TO THOSE INTERESTED IN MAGIC AND THE KINDRED ARTS

The Society of American Magicians, of which Houdini is President, is the largest magical organization of its kind in the world, with a membership of more than 1,000. Its Headquarters are in New York with branch assemblies in all principal cities. All persons, 17 years of age or more, who are interested in magic as professionals or amateurs, are eligible to membership. For particulars, address the Secretary, R. Van Dien, 230 Union Street, Jersey City, New Jersey.

INFORMATION DESIRED

HOUDINI will appreciate any information regarding experiences, for and against spiritualism. Please address him at this theatre or to 278 West 113th Street, N. Y. C.

Houdini's challenges to mediums and his explanations of dark-room deceptions infuriated psychics, delighted theatregoers.

changed into pairs of birds, animals, and a live girl. He also experimented with Buatier de Kolta's "Vanishing Lady," and a German device that made it appear a young woman, dressed as a moth, could fly about the stage.

Eventually he realized that the size of the apparatus had little to do with audience reaction. He could get more applause with his needle trick than with the Vanishing Elephant. When something disappeared, spectators wondered where it had gone; there was nothing on the stage except the performer to generate applause. A series of productions, however, heightened response. The applause grew louder each time another unexpected object appeared.

Houdini chose for his first feat "A Whirlwind of Colors," the silk spectacle he had introduced at the Hippodrome. To close the magic portion of the program, he would revive an illusion he had seen as a boy in Milwaukee—Dr. Lynn's "Paligenesia"—cutting a man into pieces, then restoring him.

Then he had a sudden inspiration. He sent two of his new dress suits to his tailor and asked him to make certain alterations.

The Houdini show opened in Pittsburgh on the evening of September 14, 1925, at the Shubert Alvin Theatre. The house lights dimmed; the orchestra played "Pomp and Circumstance"; somewhere backstage a clock struck twelve. Two young women in colonial costumes entered from the sides of the stage; they grasped the gold tassels on the blue front curtains and drew them aside. Houdini walked quickly from the wings. No one in the audience would ever shout, "It's up your sleeve," after one of his feats. He ripped off the snap-fastened sleeves of both his coat and his dress shirt, and performed with arms bare to the elbows.

Silk streamers spiraled up from the liquid-filled fishbowl. A burning lamp disappeared from one table; appeared on another. Money came from nowhere. The arm, leg, and head of a male assistant were severed, then replaced. Houdini escaped from the Water Torture Cell. The séance-room deceptions of Margery and other mediums were revealed. He offered a prize of ten thousand dollars to any psychic who could perform a single supernormal marvel that he was unable to duplicate or explain.

The tour scored a success from the start. The *Cincinnati Commercial Tribune* said: "Houdini manages these magic shows just a bit better than anyone else." The *Dayton Herald* critic noted: "Last season Thurston presented a remarkable entertainment. But Houdini captivated this reviewer in a much greater measure than his predecessor in magic."

The line at the box office at the Academy of Music in Baltimore on opening night extended from the lobby out into the street and a half block away. The *Sun* reported: "The entertainment, like Mr. Houdini himself, is a

Detachable sleeves made it clear to audiences that his hands,
not concealed devices, were responsible for Houdini's magic.

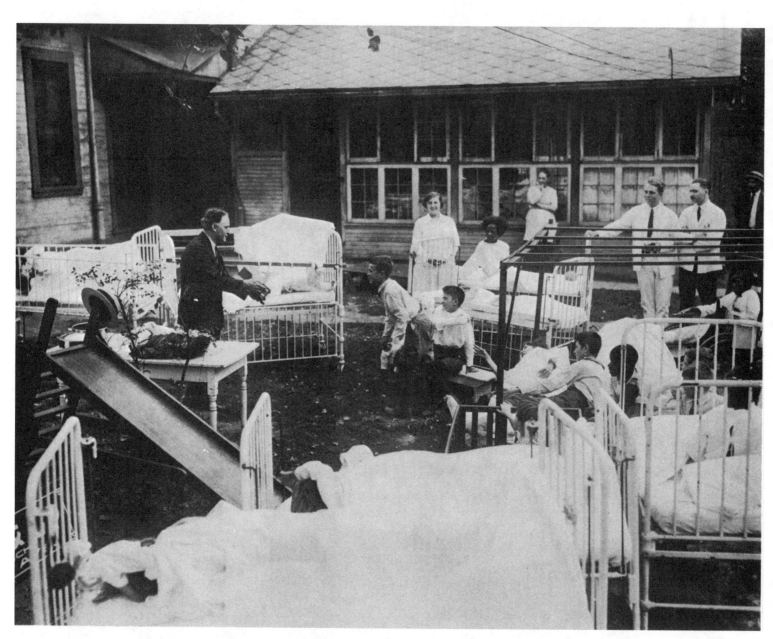

Even when on tour with his full-evening production,
Houdini found time to entertain children in hospitals.

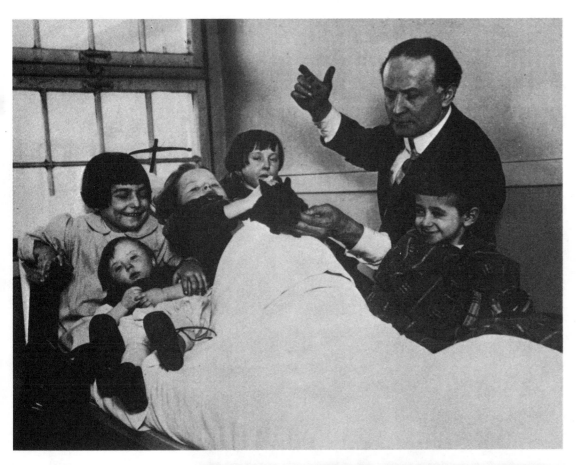

Other magicians invariably worked with white rabbits, Houdini sometimes produced one that was black.

The youngest members of the Roosevelt family and a favorite magician.

Houdini, while locked in the box he had built for Margery, could ring the bell.

Houdini stressed that his production for the road was "3 shows in 1."

The needle trick continued to be as effective as it had been years before.

Rabbits were easier to transport and house than an elephant.

At 52, Houdini had not lost his skill as a manipulator of playing cards.

vibrant testimony to the fact that the hand is quicker than the eye. . . . [He] proves spiritualistic bell ringers as bogus as the Wonderful Wizard of Oz."

Houdini varied the magic routine frequently. In Philadelphia the show opened with the replica of Robert-Houdin's Crystal Casket. The production of a girl from a super-size radio was added. The Flight of Time—vanishing and reappearing alarm clocks—closed the first act. There, as in other cities, Houdini's demonstrations of séance trickery and his challenge to psychics created a furor.

Max Holden reviewing the show in *The Sphinx*, then the most important magic magazine, said: "The spiritualistic part of the entertainment" was "worth many, many times the price of admission . . . an education for every one."

The show played a single week in most cities, but the run extended to three in Philadelphia, four in New York, and eight in Chicago. When it closed for the summer, Houdini summed up the season succinctly: "36 weeks and all O.K."

The following July, Rahman Bey, a bearded, twenty-six-year-old fakir, survived after being sealed in a metal box and lowered beneath the water of the Dalton Hotel swimming pool in New York for an hour. Hereward Carrington, who presented the fakir to the press, said there was only enough air in the container to sustain a human being for a fraction of this time. According to Carrington, the fakir performed his feat by entering a trance state, in which his circulation and respiration ceased.

Asked for his opinion, Houdini, the arch-enemy of charlatans, stated bluntly that Rahman Bey was a fraud; the alleged trance of the fakir did not account for his success. Challenged to repeat the feat himself, the magician experimented, then accepted.

On August 5, before Houdini was sealed in a metal box the same size as the one Bey used, the fifty-two-year-old magician said those who claimed a man would suffocate in three minutes were wrong. He would prove that catalepsy was not necessary for survival. There was, of course, always the possibility of an accident. If he died, however, it would be "the will of God" and his "own foolishness."

Never one to take unnecessary chances, Houdini had installed both a telephone and a signal bell in the container, so he could communicate with Collins, his principal assistant.

After being submerged an hour, the length of the fakir's stay, Houdini told Collins he would attempt to set a new record. Fifteen minutes later, he reported a slight leak. Some water had been seeping in but not enough to be dangerous yet. A minute past the hour-and-a-half mark, Houdini phoned

Detecting the method used by Argamasilla, a young Spanish psychic, to "see through" solid metal, Houdini added a version of this stunt to his close-up repertoire.

Construction and repair of stage equipment took place in Houdini's workshop.

Collins to bring him up. The magician was dripping wet and almost exhausted when tinsmiths ripped off a portion of the lid. He took several deep breaths, flexed his muscles, then announced he felt fine.

Houdini explained the technique he had used. With it people accidentally trapped in mine shafts or submarines with a limited supply of air could survive longer than had previously been thought possible. He had breathed deeply, filling his lungs, until the lid of the box was soldered shut. He then lay resting full-length flat on his back in the interior, banishing fear from his mind. He moved as little as he could, conserving oxygen by breathing rhythmically with short intakes of air.

Editorial page comments following Houdini's triumph at the Hotel Shelton pool delighted the mystifier. The *New York Herald Tribune* called him "A Dispeller of Humbug" and said:

> It detracts nothing from the admiration of Mr. Houdini's astonishing feats that he is continually demonstrating that there is nothing supernatural about them. He has performed very great services by proving that the pretensions of mediums of various sorts were false and destroying their hold on the credulous portion of the public.

The Memphis *News Scimitar* stated: "Houdini bids fair to attain high rank as one of the country's most valued citizens." Senator Arthur Capper's essay on "The Indispensible Houdini" in the *Topeka Daily Capital* recalled that the eminent magician "during the furor over ectoplasm when even notables in science were taken in . . . blew up the works by duplicating the feats of spiritualists." Capper added: "Nobody can take Houdini's place in these expositions, since he has not only the courage to try anything, but the long experience in 'magic' which has trained him to see thru what to others is an impenetrable mystery."

Before the road show began its second season in September, Houdini bought a $2,500 bronze casket and added it to his gear. Rather than exhausting himself with strenuous upside-down straitjacket escapes over city streets and risking drowning during releases from challenge packing cases submerged in rivers, he planned to publicize his show by resting in the galvanized iron box as it was submerged in water or by lying motionless in the new casket when it was interred beneath the earth.

Houdini told reporters he planned to perform from coast to coast, to make a farewell tour of the world, and then retire. He looked forward to a more leisurely life, studying the thousands of volumes he had acquired on all phases of deception, writing occasional books, and lecturing for a few weeks each year.

Houdini's library included rare books on conjuring, the theatre, occultism, and crime.

More volumes cluttered other rooms, even his private office.

Some of his treasures had been found on his last visit to Paris.

In October, while the show was in Providence, Mrs. Houdini suffered a severe attack of ptomaine poisoning. The physician summoned by her husband prescribed medicine, rest, and constant care. A nurse, who had attended Bess during previous illnesses, came from New York to stay with her, and to travel with the show until she recovered.

A hasty business trip by a slow night train to New York City fatigued Houdini before his opening performance in Albany. That night a sudden accidental jerk on the lines that were to haul up the stocks, locked around his ankles for the Water Torture Cell escape, broke a bone in his left ankle. Despite the pain, Houdini informed the audience that he would change from his bathing suit to evening clothes, then present the last act of the production. The mediumistic tricks were shown while he was seated, avoiding pressure as much as possible on the fracture.

Later, emergency-room attendants at Memorial Hospital took X rays to locate the point of the break, then applied bandages and a splint. Before going to sleep in his hotel room that night, Houdini constructed a brace for his injured leg.

The show traveled on to Schenectady, then to Montreal. Houdini continued to perform. The morning after the opening night at the Princess Theatre, he lectured for the Canadian police. That afternoon he spoke on charlatans and psychic fraud at McGill University. He ended his long day with an after-show, late-night radio interview.

Houdini arrived at the Princess Theatre an hour before noon on Friday, October 22. He was behind on his correspondence, and he expected a visitor, a student who had sketched him during his talk at McGill. The artist sat with a friend backstage in the magician's dressing room and began blocking out a portrait.

Another student from McGill returned a book he had borrowed from Houdini, then stayed to ask several questions as the artist continued his work. Was it true Houdini could sustain punches to his midsection without injury? The magician, relaxing on a couch, more interested in reading the morning's mail than replying, extended his arm and invited the visitor to feel the powerful muscles. The student asked if he could take a few trial punches. Houdini, looking up, said yes. The visitor, not realizing that Houdini had to brace himself, struck him immediately. Two quick jabs followed the first blow. The artist and his friend, thinking the young man had gone berserk, were about to jump up and restrain him when the magician himself signaled for a halt.

After the visitors left, Houdini became increasingly conscious of a pain in his stomach. Every move he made on the stage that night seemed to intensify the dull ache in his broken ankle and the burning sensation in his mid-

The last tricked "spirit" photograph of Houdini in 1926.

Three portraits of the master mystifier
as he appeared in his later years.

The last theatrical picture of Houdini, made in the fall of 1926.

section. He mentioned his discomfort to no one. He had had aches and pains before. The less he thought about them, the quicker they healed.

Houdini gave his last show in Montreal Saturday night, then boarded the train for Detroit, where he was to open the next evening, before telling his wife what had happened Friday in his dressing room. By then the pain was too intense to hide.

Still weak from her own illness, Bess collapsed. When the train made a brief stop at London, Ontario, a telegram was dispatched to the show's advance publicity man. He was to have the best doctor in Detroit waiting at the Statler Hotel, ready to give Houdini a thorough examination.

The train arrived very late. Rather than going first to their hotels, the entire company went directly to the Garrick Theatre. Houdini pitched in and helped his assistants and the stagehands set up his equipment.

Meanwhile Dr. Leo Dretzka and the advance man were waiting in the Statler lobby. In an hour or so, the physician had to leave for a medical convention in Canada. Finally, after asking a dozen times at the desk if the magician had sent any message, the advance man called the theatre.

There was no cot in Houdini's dressing room at the Garrick. He stripped off his clothes and stretched out on the floor. Dr. Dretzka knelt and touched the inflamed abdomen. Bess was not in the room; she did not hear the physician say her husband was suffering from acute appendicitis, that he should be admitted to a hospital at once.

The theatre manager stopped by to report that the house was sold out. Houdini began dressing for the show. "They're here to see me," he explained as the worried doctor rushed off to catch his train. "I won't disappoint them."

The performance started thirty minutes late. "We have just made a thousand-mile journey from Montreal, and we are tired," Houdini explained; then he ripped off his sleeves and began the hour-long first act. Only once did he vary the routine. The flourish of his arm as he whirled the silk from the fishbowl sent flames of pain to his stomach. He stepped aside; Collins, his chief assistant, understood. He whipped out the yards and yards of streamers, then the long string of flags.

The smile left Houdini's face the moment the curtains closed. He staggered and fell. He was carried to his dressing room. His temperature had reached 104 degrees; perspiration poured from his face and body. Through sheer will power, he forced himself to return to the stage following the intermission. He collapsed again after the final curtain, but still refusing to heed the physician's advice went to the Statler Hotel.

Bess knew there was only one way to handle her stubborn husband; she had hysterics. Not, however, until Dr. Daniel E. Cohn, the hotel's physi-

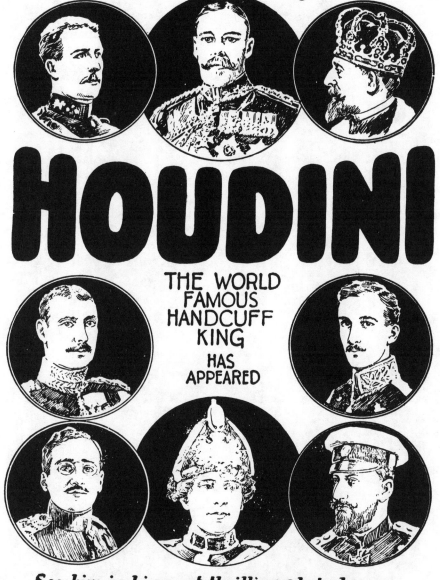

Before the Crowned Heads of Europe and other world famous personages

HOUDINI

THE WORLD
FAMOUS
HANDCUFF
KING

HAS
APPEARED

Houdini did not perform for many of the people pictured in this advertisement for his film.

See him in his most thrilling photodrama~

"HALDANE OF THE SECRET SERVICE"

The Water Torture Cell in the 1952 Paramount film, starring Tony Curtis, did not look like the one Houdini used.

The Houdini jail escapes were performed in the nude, not while he was clothed as shown in the Paramount movie.

The under-a-frozen-river episode in the Paramount movie *Houdini* never occurred during his career.

James Randi verified the master escapologist's statement that there was enough air in the coffin for survival in February 1956.

Randi was submerged for an hour and forty-five minutes at the Shelton pool.

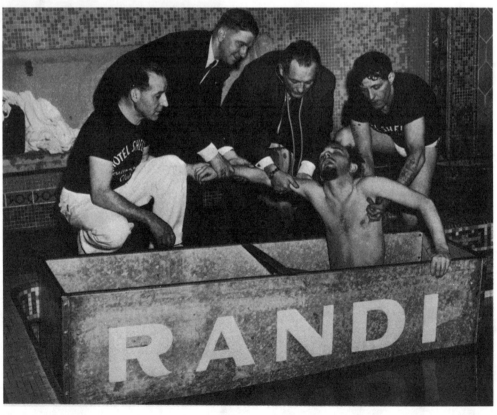

Stuart Damon starred as Houdini in *Man of Magic*, a London musical, in November 1966.

Milbourne Christopher re-created one of Houdini's performances of fifty years before in *Houdini—Magic versus The Occult* at Lincoln Center, New York, in March 1976.

Damon escaped from handcuffs, a trunk, and a water torture cell.

cian; Dr. Charles K. Kennedy, a specialist who arrived at 3 A.M.; and the magician's own physician, Dr. William Stone, reached in New York by telephone, warned that he would die without treatment—did Houdini enter Grace Hospital. There his ruptured appendix was removed. Four days later, when streptococcus peritonitis developed, a second operation was performed. To no avail. On Sunday afternoon, October 31, 1926— Halloween—at twenty-six minutes past one, Houdini died.

Before he died, the man whom *The Literary Digest* called "the greatest necromancer of the age—perhaps of all times" had said he would send a message to his wife from beyond the grave, if this was possible.

In 1929 his widow—who recently had injured her head falling down a flight of stairs, who was under a doctor's care, and who had been having hallucinations—thought she heard Houdini speaking through the Reverend Arthur Ford, a medium. When she recovered her health, she disavowed this communication. Thereafter Bess continued to state until she died that she had never received an authentic message.

Many séances were held in various parts of the world, but no one heard Houdini's voice—until July 1, 1970. Shortly past noon on that day, Dr. George N. Gordon, director of the Hofstra University Communications Center; David Rea, a producer, then working on a Houdini documentary for BBC-TV; Rea's secretary; Arthur Leroy, a magician who had known Houdini; and the present writer assembled in Thomas Alva Edison's laboratory at the Edison Historic Site in West Orange, New Jersey.

Several old phonograph cylinders, once owned by the master mystifier, had been found in the collection of the late John Mulholland, a distinguished magician and one of Houdini's friends.

Soon after one of the cylinders was inserted in the proper machine, we heard these words through the metal horn: "Ladies and gentlemen, I take great pleasure in introducing my latest invention—the Water Torture Cell."

Houdini went on to say that there was "nothing supernatural" about the feat. When the cell was filled with water, it would be "absolutely impossible" for a person locked inside to have access to air.

He described in detail every part of the cell, the wooden stocks, and the steel grille, which when lowered into the water would prevent him from turning right side up, even if he could free his ankles from the stocks. If an emergency arose, one of his assistants would be ready with an axe to smash the glass front of the cell to save him from drowning. He did not think this would be necessary "but we all know accidents will happen—and when least expected."

There was another version of this speech on the cylinder that followed.

The original bust of Houdini at his grave was destroyed by vandals.
It was replaced in 1976 by the Society of American Magicians.

On a third, Houdini introduced his sister Gladys. After she recited a poem their father had written in German, Houdini said that to make sure everyone understood the words, he would repeat the verses himself. He pronounced each syllable as clearly as if he were speaking from the stage of the New York Hippodrome.

When and where had these recordings been made? The magician answered this question himself: "Harry Houdini, October 29, 1914, Flatbush, New York."

More than fifty years have passed since the master mystifier gave his last performance in Detroit. Séances are still being held on the anniversary of his death, but it is most unlikely that Houdini, or anyone else, will communicate from the Great Beyond. If, however, there should be a breakthrough in the future, the odds are it will be made by the dynamic showman who convinced the world that he could escape from anything.

CAN HOUDINI SAM GET LOOSE?
HARRY MURPHY + T.B. in The CHICAGO HERALD & EXAMINER.
Copyright, 1922 by Star Company

APPENDIX

Written in 1917 before *The Master Mystery*, Houdini's film serial, was produced, *The Marvelous Adventures of Houdini, the Justly Celebrated Elusive American* contains elements later used in the motion pictures made by the Houdini Film Corporation.

The books he prepared for the public were edited. This unrevised scenario is pure Houdini.

The Marvelous Adventures of

HOUDINI

The Justly Celebrated Elusive American

By Harry Houdini.

Price for copy, One Dollar. Apply for copies to HARRY HOUDINI, 394 East 21st Street, Flatbush, Brooklyn, New York.

HOUDINI

————

CAST OF CHARACTERS.

Harry Houdini..Harry Houdini, as known to the Public.

Beulah.........Leading lady, is recognized by all beholders as the personification of refinement, has traveled much with retentative brain is at ease in the highest society in London, a welcome guest of Nobility in Germany, has lived in Hong-Kong, and knows the thoroughfares of the capitals without looking at the streets or asking questions
She is still a girl, yet possesses the poise and understanding beyond her years. As Cicero would say, "A little of an old woman in a young woman." Beulah still retains her girlish traits, a girlish woman, or rather a womanly girl, one whose affections would spring from a mental attraction, rather than from a physical or sex magnet. She is not a hero worshipper.

June ....Ingenue. Like her birth month, is sunshine, youth and happiness.

one

Jimmy.........Juvenile. A boy who would be in love with sunshine and to whom nothing is so rare as June.

Siddons........Chief of Secret Government Police. Such a man as would be selected by the brain force of a great nation, to have complete control of the Secret Service, in fact a prototype of Flynn,—suave, polished, a gentleman, and silent as the Sphinx.

Cobb...........Heavy. A world's Diplomat, a worthy opponent for Houdoni. Physically ready for battle; mentally a feared power among strategists.

Evora..........Heavy. Woman. The Latin type; flashing physical attractiveness, a frequenter of Monte Carlo, woman of the world, who lives by her wits, and with her manners manages to gain entree into the inner circles of Society.

It has been the custom for years in Atlantic City for the Fourth of July week to bring the biggest and best drawing headliner to all the theatres, and, when B. F. Keith's Circuit obtained the Million Dollar Pier, they never were approached with their attractions.

For the past few years, Houdini, known all over the world as The Elusive American, was the attraction, and combined with his out-door challenges, it was universally granted that for the Big Fourth of July week, Houdini was accepted as The Big Affair, in fact it was conceded that when he arrived it was the Mardi Gras of Mystery Week, and everyone awaited with bated breath for notification what hazardous challenge he would be asked to accept, for there were always some

two

committee of challengers who knew they could defeat him.

In the past few years, they had buried him alive in the sands, manacled. Then he had been encased into a chain bag and now it was expected that the Police Department were going to challenge him to escape from all of their irons trussed up in a helpless condition, and he was to be thrown overboard from the Pier.

His arrival was looked for; the opening night. as usual, the house was sold out, hundreds were unable to gain admission. His receiption really an ovation, and during his work, a box-party were unusually demonstrative. The box-party was a celebration affair given by Cid Cobb, a world's diplomat, a mental giant who would not stop at anything to obtain his point, Evora, an associate and confident; the flashy dark-eyed Latin type with sinuous movements reminding one of the movements of a serpent, beautiful but deadly.

Beulah, a woman who is recognized immediately as one who has traveled much and well; who is welcomed in London, has a home in Paris and can find her way around Tien Tsien or Bombay without an interpreter.

June, seated alongside Jimmy, and both being watched with an amused look by the girl's father, Siddons, Chief of the Secret Service.

All during the action of Houdini's performance, the suspense is of such a nature that the entire house was hushed, but in the private box, the Chief, knowing Houdini has conquered all his pet handcuffs, looks on, knowing that anything Houdini would accept in the form of a challenge or feat, never having been defeated, it was only a very remote chance that Houdini could be uncrowned.

three

In the midst of his act, Houdini walked down to the footlights and announced that he had received a letter from the Police Department and that he had accepted their challenge, to be heavily manacled; weighted down with chains and that they would throw him overboard, but only under the condition that if he accepted he must sign a form, that in case any accident were to transpire, they could not be held accountable.

Remarking that he was willing to sign and he would accept the challenge for the next day between the hours of 12 and one o'clock, test to take place at the end of the Million Dollar Pier.

During the announcement, Beulah had been listening with awe in her face, staring so intently at Houdini that Houdini must have felt the gaze and without seeking to look into the box, he turned sideways and encountered the gaze of Beulah.

An understanding seems to have been reached, and he, who had never looked into a woman's eyes, stood for a moment as if transfixed, recovering himself, he went on with his performance.

Beulah could not understand, she seemed stunned and after a few moments, though all the others had risen, and were ready to leave, asked Chief Siddons, if they could meet Houdini. With pleasure, the party are taken to Houdini's dressing room and formally introduced, takes them to the end of pier, showing them from which portion he will be thrown, so that Siddons can have his launch in position the next day, to be able to see the entire proceedings.

Beulah who has been listening to Houdini talk, seemed entranced, her heart beating rapidly, to think he would brave death the next day and seem so unconcerned. She asks him if he has no one at home to stop him, no home that must compel him

four

to be careful. Houdini registers the fact he has no one at home, his home is called Playground for his work, is his play. Beulah has a beautiful home in Florida, describes same to Houdini, especially with the flowers in front of her home, growing in the landscape gardening "HOME" being planted in the front lawn in great big letters, with a large clock with small flowers growing in the handle, so that all time is flowery, remarking that there is no time like the present, and "While we live let us live."

The next day the beach is packed with the holiday multitude, who have arrived to see Houdini go overboard, bathing girls in abundance, male swimmers, swimming around, in fact, at least ten thousand on the beach and being Fourth of July week, the crowds are countless. All kinds of crafts have gathered, from the enlarged sized "old oaken bucket" boat skulled with a broken oar, to the Millionaire's Yacht.

Our box-party arrive in Cobb's Yacht, and watch the proceedings of the six policemen, who are now manacling Houdini, all being elevated on a platform easily seen by the entire crowd.

Beulah manages to obtain a nod or recognition from Houdini and that is the only sign Houdini gives during the entire test, for he is intently watching the manner and style of manacling he is receiving, watching carefully, so that he will know how to start, when once below the surface.

After trussing him up, like a refractory prisoner, the police take him, toss him overboard, Houdini sinks like a plummet to the bottom of the ocean and releases himself, coming to the surface free from his incumbrances, holding a few handcuffs in his hands, swims toward the shore followed by hundreds of bathers, as soon as his feet

five

touch the land, he is grabbed, and hoisted to the shoulders of the admiring mob, shoulder high and taken to his dressing room, which is at the end of the Million Dollar pier.

Chief Siddon invites Houdini to lunch on the Yacht, launch arriving for that purpose, he accepts and joins the lunch party, among the party are a number of foreign representatives who in the course of conversation being informed of Houdini's Diving suit, became greatly interested, and Cobb who before has only looked on Houdini as an entertainer, now makes advances to become his friend.

As Houdini's diving suit has not been seen in any public demonstration, and hearing that it is one that can be used in deep water and in case of danger the only one that the diver could assist himself in case of danger, he wishes to obtain possession by right of purchase, but Houdini states that he is about to make the final tests before presenting to the United States Government.

Cobb informs Houdini that his Government has lost a lot of divers, who, on their efforts to salvage valuable cargo by the extra sharp coral reefs, the diver either having his life line cut, or being caught with the leaden shoes in places the coral permitting the unfortunate to sink waist high, and never being able to extract his feet, from which position it was impossible to rescue him, so the work was given up. At all events, Houdini refuses to show the diving suit, and that he must make final test in private waters as all his tests have been made in tanks, now he must try it in free water.

Cobb explains they are going to Beulah's home in Florida, why not join. Houdini refuses, but when Beulah joins in the entreaties, says he will

six

go, and that he will take his assistants with him, if that is acceptable, he will join the party.

On board the Yacht, Houdini's assistants arrive. Baggage and Diving suit, which is completely covered, only the regulation Government helmet showing, so no one knows exactly what it really looks like; nor what it is supposed to do.

Two of Houdini's assistants, Collins and Penridg, they work together, but always seem to find something to argue over, in fact, it is an endless chain of arguments, but when it comes to work, they work together like one unit. They are loyal to Houdini, in fact, are a typical Damon and Pythias. Scenes can be imagined, wherein they are in deadly combat, but at a word from Houdini they will be seen helping each other out of predicaments. They can be shown though fighting all the time, that their hearts are as far from fraud, as heaven is from hell.

The Yacht starts away, Jimmy and June are in love with each other, Cobb resents this and tries to force his attentions on June, who is all eyes for Jimmy, he being more of her style.

Evora, does not like the idea of Cobb trying to win out June, shows her hatred for the girl and manages to trip her up, causing June to fall overboard. Jimmy sees the girl overboard, dives to save her, not being experienced, not knowing that he must keep away from the graps of a drowning person, June clutches him holding him helpless. Excitement on board the yacht, they sink twice, at the third time, Houdini comes on scene, kicking off shoes, dives overboard, swims to drowning couple, gets behind Jimmy, rips up the coat, ties the coat-tails into a knot, puts it over his neck and holds up the couple until assistance arrives. Evora being the first to render aid to poor June after her experience, showing hypocrisy.

seven

During the voyage, Beulah and Houdini have become better acquainted, though Houdini walks alone all the time, Beulah watching him from her steamer chair; not understanding, for the heart has reasons that the reason cannot understand.

It can here be registered Houdini work place, a large log hut, with workshop attachments, place can be called "Lake of Peace" and flashback if required, Houdini surrounded by his assistants working.

Beulah: "You don't talk much, Mr. Houdini."

Houdini: "No speech was given to mankind to conceal their thoughts, it is better to fall among crows than flatterers, for crows devour only the dead—flatterers the living."

Beulah: "You are pessimistic—time will cure all."

Houdini: "No hand can make the clock strike for me, the hours that have passed."

Once in a while Houdini gazes at Beulah in a thoughtful manner.

The yacht reaches Florida, Beulah's home shown. Jimmy and June arm in arm on deck, Cobb is seen secretly trying to open door with false key, the diving suit, is in this room. Houdini's assistant catches Cobb, "Wrong room very sorry", Houdini's assistants show suspicion.

Party disembarks, Beulah turns smiling as she points to her home, with the word Home in flowers on the front lawn. "Welcome home, Mr. Houdini." "Home"—murmurs Houdini, "Yes, it is a home." Since his folks have passed away he has had no home, there was no one living in his heart of hearts, but looking at her, his heart spoke a language strong in its appeal, that thrilled him through and through, swaying his senses. It was all so strange to him, that only a sight of Beulah seemed to relieve him.

eight

They walk together up the flowered path, he looking around, and eventually looking in her eyes, she turns away (this could be a flash back later on). Big American flag in background or on top of her home fluttering in the breeze.

Days pass, Houdini is now preparing for the final test of diving suit. Houdini and Beulah enter speed boat, to inform United States Officials to witness test and borrow maps, while his assistants prepare things, i. e., get diving suit into a launch so some work can be done on same. Two assistants remain on yacht, one Vickery, the only one on boat with Diving suit.

Cobb and Elvora seen in motor boat. Elvora seated and Cobb on end of boat ready to step on shore. Vickery seems to forget something, goes to house or garage, Cobb runs to boat to get diving suit, when Jimmy and June appear on scene, not knowing what is happening, board the launch, Cobb hurriedly hides himself, and when they are out a little way, dips his handkerchief, Elvora sees signal, follows. Cobb overpowers Jimmy, locks him in the cabin of the launch. Elvora by this time reaches them, June is forced into the Elvora boat. Cobb steals the diving suit, then takes out the plug at bottom of the other boat, skuttling it, with Jimmy locked into the cabin.

Exit Elvora, June and Cobb with the diving suit, the launch with Jimmy sinks. He tries to batter down the door, he tries to smash the porthole glass, which he eventually does, but is too small for him to exit, he waves his hand, grasping a towel, interior scene can be seen where he is slowly being covered with water, and eventually the launch sinks below the surface of the ocean. Houdini through a telescope notices the launch sink, heads toward it, arrives. The launch now

nine

being below surface, Houdini rapidly divests himself of some clothes, but being ready for diving test he can be underdressed, or even appear with a robe, with which he has gone on speed boat with Beulah. He dives under water, swims about—finds launch, sees the hand through port-hole. Swims toward door, finds it locked, comes to surface to get "something" from his robe or clothes, dives down again, picks lock open, drags out Jimmy and brings him to surface. Beulah helps both into launch, Jimmy is almost "out" but is helped to full senses, they return to Beulah's home. Jimmy relating full story of theft of diving suit and capture of June. Arrival at Beulah's home. She says" Good-bye, remember this is always home, we never turn any one away."

Houdini sends Beulah to inform Siddons what has occurred and to bring aid.

In the mean time Cobb, with Elvora and June on the yacht, which they have reached from the motor boat with diving suit are speeding into the open sea, toward Felice Island, a Government in which Cobb is one of the head officials, Chief of a cunning band of smugglers, rich, having grown powerful and very rich with their successful submarine methods in smuggling, being almost immune from capture or discovery, as the ordinary ship could not pass through the coral reefs and there happened to be a path leading the reefs, through which a submarine could easily find its way. As long as a light ship passed in high tide, they were safe, if knowing the route, and their Yacht was built with special flat bottom not to take in too deep water. Through a field glass Cobb watches Houdini in speed boat with Jimmy, June stealthily lowers knotted rope over side. Speed boat approaches, Cobb orders it sunk, fires, hits

ten

speed boat, the momentum causes it to almost get alongside same, as they flounder in the sea. Jimmy manages to get get hold of rope, through porthole. Houdini tries to imitate the rope climbing feat when he is almost to the top, Cobb cuts the rope, and Houdini falls back into the sea. He manages to grasp the rudder, and is seen being dragged behind yacht into the open sea.

June from opposite side throws out life preserver, lashed to a long rope, Houdini watches the life preserver, sees June's hand and sleeve, knows it is all right, clutches the rope, manages to get on board, helpless. He is captured by crew of Cobb, and while in a helpless condition Houdini is strapped into a straight-jacket, he is carried to a room, Cobb kicks Houdini, when Houdini is lying down, and Cobb, to make the straps tighter takes off his coat, leaving it on back of chair.

The two assistants of Houdini are in some place bound and gagged they have been captured, when Collins left boat they had remained on board the yacht.

Houdini manages to get into coat pocket with his foot and with pencil between toes, writes them a code message, to get near him.

Houdini is now taken from the cabin by Cobb and the crew, and lashed by his feet, still in the straight-jacket from which he has not been given time to try and effect his escape. He is hung head foremost from the yard-arm ''Food for the Sea Gulls'', if they want a change of diet.

They leave Houdini hanging in mid-air, after watching him a few moments, Jimmy tries to help Houdini, cannot do so, but watches Houdini eventually free himself, from straight-jacket, free his ankles, and drop into the sea. Last seen of Hou-

eleven

dini, the yacht is sailing away, and Houdini swimming slowly out of sight. He manages to find a board on which he is thrown by surf on shore of a tribe of tree dwellers, a cruel mob with whom might is right.

In the meanwhile, the Cobb Yacht arrives at their destination, Felice Island, they take June and Jimmy, lock them into their prison.

Felice having been very prosperous, is the most modern island, they having their own electric plants and telephone, for Honolulu is one of the best-equipped islands in the world, far ahead of Australia where in Brisbane and Queensland they have no hygienic appliances, even in the first-class hotels. Whereas an island like Honolulu is fully equipped and has the finest natural automobile road in the world.

Houdini is thrown on shore, is spied by the natives, who are about to prepare their annual sacrifice, who have been dancing around, heathenish ways, religious rites, and a slow upraising of hands, and bowing to the earth.

Their King or leader, Nala, a giant negro type, bedecked with human teeth as a necklace, the skulls of his vanquished foes slung around his waist, these skulls are heavily loaded with loadstone to keep evil spirits away, he approaches Houdini, and calling his council together informs them that they will not sacrifice one of their own, but this being a white human, it will be a better sacrifice.

Houdini is taken, the poor savage they have had strung in the air is removed, and Houdini is spread in the air, with ropes and fire about to be lit, when they commence their devotions, Houdini manages to release himself, freeing first his hands, he sways, hanging by his feet, and lands

twelve

in their midst. Recaptured, Nala says "This man is not for God's on high, but for the Demons of the Deep."

There is an old broken ship's anchor, Houdini is lashed to this, carried onto a catamaran, all the natives following in their boats, canoes, tree, logs, and when out a little way, Nala orders Houdini overboard, this is done, and they commence their devotions, Nala standing erect with his hands in supplication to the High Gods, this is the way his tribe see him as they throw themselves prostrate.

Houdini sinks with the anchor to the bottom, releases himself, and in coming up, Nala has slowly prostrated himself, but so that he is "graspable" by Houdini, who reaches up to get a hold onto catamaran, sees Nala, grabs him by the human teeth necklace and pulls him overboard.

Now ensues a death struggle under water the like never seen before by human eye.

In this, the skulls around Nala's waist sink the two battling men-fish to the bottom, each tries to break the other's hold, Nala manages to get Houdini around the throat, and is forcing him away (right against the vision of the spectator) and the battle royal continues, wrestling against each other, showing the skill of both men as swimmers, eventually Houdini, who has been trying to get away from the grasp of the negro-giant, gets his foot into the string of skulls, breaks the string, skulls sink away and both struggling men are carried to the top, on the way up Houdini manages to get a knee hold around Nala's neck, raises himself and is thus first to get to the surface, he grasps the catamaran with his hands, is thus enabled to keep Nala under water, disposing of this fierce opponent, who sinks below.

thirteen

Houdini gets onto the catamaran and assumes the position that Nala held before he drew him over to his watery grave, the natives arise, see Houdini there posing instead of their King, frightened scene, they all dive overboard and away to shore, leaving Houdini monarch of all he surveys.

Houdini picks up a big paddle dropped by one of the natives and floats out to the open sea.

With tide and paddle Houdini manages to get to an island, enters harbor, as he gets in he recognizes the Cobb yacht, he reconnoitres. Men are loading the yacht preparing evidently for a long voyage.

A large crane on dock, through this agency, the yacht is being loaded with boxes, it swings from dock to yacht. Houdini get on dock, wants to get on board unseen. They have brought a piano, placed it into a piano box, as they are nailing it up, they leave a side loose, Houdini manages to get into this, they come back, renail it, heavily rope same, sling chain on it, and are going to put it on the yacht. As the box is swung in mid-air, piano, Houdini and all, the crane being overloaded, it falls outwards. Houdini is thrown with piano overboard (in plain view) and being weighted by the heavy chain sinks overboard and manages to make his escape.

As piano box is falling, through a hole Houdini keeps waving his hand, by this sign, we know positively that he is inside. He escapes in Houdini fashion!

Houdini swims up, manages to get himself on yacht, finds his two assistants again quarreling. They scheme to regain diving suit by capturing submarine and get away, this being the only way it is possible for them to do so.

fourteen

Houdini gets suit of clothes, a naval uniform complete, walks the rope to shore, steals an electric car (having heard that June and Jimmy were in jail), goes to prison, scales the high wall, climbs up in human fly fashion, overpowers guard, Houdini having on uniform of the yacht, guards permit him to get close until too late and he overpowers them. Houdini frees June and Jimmy, gets them to the top of wall, through the window, it being too far to jump or drop, Houdini gets a firm hock hold of window, jumps to wire, a deliberate jump, grasps hands of Jimmy, swings him to a tree, lands him safe, grasps hands of June, swings her to Jimmy, they descend, get into the car and in the rush and excitement going down a hill, Houdini hits a stone, on top of a hill, knocks Houdini off electric car saves himself, grabbing roots, but electric car keeps right on going with its occupants overboard with a splash and to the bottom of the sea.

Houdini sees the car sinking, dives overboard, opens door, June and Jimmy have been knocked senseless, he arrives at surface with June, finds Jimmy not here, dives back and saves Jimmy. The car runs along the bottom of the ocean and Houdini has to swim after it, there being an electric motor in car.

June helps Houdini carry Jimmy into an old warehouse by side of the hill and discover to their surprise that it is a sort of a hotel for extra crews of the smugglers. Houdini lays plans for the complete submerging of the warehouse in the following manner:

He will remove all the supporting pilings of the foundation, except what are absolutely necessary for its support. These are then arranged to be destroyed at a given signal. He will cover the

fifteen

roof with dirt and stones so that it bears a strik-
ing resemblance to the surrounding territory.
Then at given signal the supports are destroyed
and the building sinks three stories so that the
covering of the roof blends with the surrounding
country on the same level. Thus the warehouse
sinks three stories and no one looking on, could
have told what became of it nor where it had
formerly stood.

No food being around, Houdini searches, fails
to find anything; on crawling along a dark passage which seems to lead to the street he looks
through and right by the passers by lane, the
window looking right on same, he finds bunches of
bananas hanging on the roof. He gets to the floor
above, finds a small hole but cannot get his hand
through; finding an umbrella and a cold chisel he
forces the umbrella through the small hole, opens
umbrella and as it is not below the length of the
banana bunches, he commences to enlarge the
hole, the debris falling into the open umbrella, so
if there are any passers by, they will not notice
any dirt or chips falling. Houdini gets the food,
returns to Jimmy and June.

He finds a couple of candles and matches and
plans to make their escape, the candles will suf-
fice to lead them through the dark passages which
Houdini has reason to believe leads them right to
the docks, to the submarine base.

To keep attention from them, he will fire the
warehouse and when all attention is towards the
warehouse, it will enable them to get into a submarine and escape.

They notice that the windows are nailed and are
permanent, in fact only being windowpanes in
solid places, Jimmy wants to break window to get
away, Houdini stops him, shows him some of the

sixteen

fly paper around; places paper on window and cuts circle with a diamond ring, breaks glass, for had the glass fallen it might attract someone, in this way the broken glass sticks to the fly paper.

The window being enlarged, lowers Jimmy and June by sheets (taken from the beds) on side of the warehouse, away from street side, they get out of window and onto a lower roof. Houdini fixes Fire Bug, spreads paper and straw, lights candles and attaches shoelaces to bell of telephone so when hammer rings, will pull candles over and start fire, planning that he will call up and start the blaze. Lights candles, June and Jimmy escape on their way to the U-53.

Houdini is so long, guard he has overpowered is found by three guards, who loosen him and on a voyage of discovery get to Houdini, capture Houdini and lash him to the chair. Jimmy and June enter submarine.

Cobb 'phones through to warehouse, is informed that Jimmy and June have escaped, calls guards from Houdini, who is now tied into the chair, they leave him to go to dock, Cobb sees U-53 submerge, in the meantime, Cobb, phoning, has overthrown candles, fire has started in the warehouse, and Houdini will be burnt to death, having fixed a death trap for himself.

He is seen trying to escape from ropes, fire enters all over, and Houdini does his world-famous rope escape that thousands of thousands have tried to ensnare him, with the fire raging around him and wriggling to escape.

He escapes, gets to window down on the water-pipe or from window to window or with his shoes off, Japanese fashion, using his big toe to hold onto the wires or cables that hold up the edge or coping in roof.

Warehouse is now made to vanish.

seventeen

Cobb orders "nets down," it will be impossible for anyone to find their way out of the submarine traps, which were built in case any nation would ever try to get to the island. He gives chase.

Jimmy and June are away in the smaller size submarine, Cobb after them in the regulation size submarine.

Houdini's two assistants in the meanwhile have loaded the diving suit into Submarine, awaiting their chief's appearance. Houdini rushes down to dock, gets into submarine, submerges and finds that he is trapped in the steel nets, not knowing his way out, he is stalled.

Being equipped with the latest devices, his submarine (if desired can be seen) rolling along on wheels, a long handle on which a steel-cutting saw is affixed and which is manipulated from the inside, this saw cuts out a portion of the steel netting and rolls through the space into the open sea and ascends.

In going up, Houdini crashes into the submarine of Cobb's, causing both submarines to sink to the bottom.

Not being able to move, Houdini is assisted into his diving suit by his two assistants, and goes into the sea, to make what repairs possible.

Cobb in the meanwhile has sent out two of his men in self-contained diving suits, they behold Houdini at work, get behind him and grapple. A subsea fight takes place, two against one, one of the divers managing to cut the life line of Houdini's diving suit and signalling to Houdini's assistants O. K., to throw them off that anything is wrong. The other diver now engages Houdini and cuts the air-tube and Houdini relies on his invention to escape, he extricates himself from his diving patent suit and battles with the two

eighteen

divers. Overcoming them, he manages to screw the face plate off one, who falls, then swimming toward the other, manages to defeat him in the same manner.

As Houdini rises to the top, he is caught amidships with the periscope of a passing submarine, he becomes entangled, he is powerless and it takes him to the top.

Houdini struggles to free himself, but fails, the submarine again descends, and Jimmy, who is guiding the submarine, not knowing what is wrong, looks through the water glass and sees Cobb's submarine.

He fires a torpedo, misses, the shock jars Houdini loose from the periscope, he swims away and finding the submarine in his way, he tries to swim under it, groping with his hands, just then Jimmy, knowing he has missed, not having felt the shock of any explosion, fires again.

This time he hits the Cobb submarine, destroying same, and Houdini gets into torpedo chute, enters the submarine, startled to find Jimmy and June, he falls exhausted into a chair, Jimmy shuts the torpedo chute, starts the engine, turning to Houdini he asks: "Where to now, Mr. Houdini." Houdini says quietly: "Home, James."

Flash back to Beulah's home.

"HOME, SWEET HOME."

nineteen

ACKNOWLEDGMENTS
AND SOURCES

Many people contributed important information during the years I gathered data on Houdini: Theodore Hardeen, Mrs. Houdini, James Collins, Mrs. Pauline Vickery, Will Goldston, B. M. L. Ernst, Mrs. Roberta Ernst, Frank Ducrot, Fredrick Eugene Powell, Dr. Henry Ridgely Evans, Howard Thurston, Dante (Harry Jansen), Fred Keating, Horace Goldin, Jean Hugard, Okito (Theodore Bamberg), Fu Manchu (David Bamberg), Fulton Oursler, Harry Blackstone, Samuel Margules, Joseph F. Rinn, Messmore Kendall, Willard Greene, John Mulholland, Arthur Leroy, John J. McManus, Jean Irving, Clayton Rawson, William Lindsay Gresham, and Lester Grimes.

I am indebted to Joseph Dunninger, Clarence Hubbard, Dr. Boris Zola, Al Flosso, Arthur Lloyd, David J. Lustig, Amedeo Vacca, Dr. and Mrs. Victor Trask, Dai Vernon, Jack Gwynne, Theo Doré, Fred Beckman, Walter B. Gibson, Clarence Blair, Carroll Bish, Edgar Heyl, C. B. Yohe, Loring Campbell, George Boston, Art Ronnie, Michael Miller, John Daniel, Hugh Riley, Arnold Furst, Bernard Rind, Lawrence Arcuri, Arnold Belais, Canon William V. Rauscher, Hen Fetsch, George Goebel, Dr. Bernard C. Meyer, and Albert Green.

I am grateful to fellow collectors who gave me access to their material: George Pfisterer, Sidney Hollis Radner, H. Adrian Smith, Tad Ware, Stanley Palm, Dr. Morris N. Young, Dr. Joseph H. Fries, Pat Culliton, Manuel Weltman, Robert Lund, Larry Weeks, Stuart Cramer, Jay Marshall, Dr. John Henry Grossman, John Booth, Lloyd E. Jones, Philip T. Thomas, Fred Rickard, Al Guenther, George McAthy, and Allen Berlinski.

Equally cooperative were Dr. Jules Dhotel, Agosta-Meynier, André Mayette, Georges Gaillard, and Michel Seldow in Paris; Jean Chavigny and Paul Robert-Houdin in Blois; Robelly in Orléans (Loire); Monarque, Klingsor, and Louis Tummers in Brussels; Peter and Jorgen Borsch and Leo Leslie Clemmensen in Copenhagen; Topper Martyn in Stockholm; Dr. Kurt Volkmann in Düsseldorf; George Armstrong, Stankey Thomas, Chris Charlton, Robert Harbin, and John Salisse in London; Roland Winder in Leeds; and J. B. Findlay in Shanklin, Isle of Wight.

Thanks are due to Herbert E. Pratt and Arthur Ivey at the Magic Circle Collection in London; A. H. Wesencraft, Harry Price Collection, University of London; Paul Meyers, New York Public Library Theatre Collection at Lincoln Center; Louis A. Rackow, John Mulholland Collection at The Players, New York City; Dr. William Van Lennep, Harvard Theatre Collection; Richard Hart, Enoch Pratt Library, Baltimore; the staffs of the Library of Congress in Washington, where Houdini and McManus-Young collections are housed, and the University of Texas at Austin, where more Houdini and McManus-Young material is available. Equipment, advertising matter, and other interesting items are on view at the Houdini Magical Hall of Fame in Niagara Falls, Canada.

The illustrations and most of the source material for this volume are in my collection in New York City. This includes Houdini letters, manuscripts, photographs, posters, scrapbooks, files of the conjuring periodicals of his day, books by and about him, apparatus, and the desk trunk Houdini shipped back to Germany from the Russian border, rather than permit custom inspectors to open it and see the notes he had made on the methods used for his sensational releases.

MILBOURNE CHRISTOPHER, 1976

BIBLIOGRAPHY

WORKS BY HOUDINI

Magic Made Easy. (Pamphlets offering secrets and equipment for sale.) New York, 1898; Chicago, 1899, published by author.

Between 1900 and 1924, souvenir booklets were published in England, the United States, and Russia bearing such titles as *America's Sensational Perplexer; Houdini; The Famous Houdini; The Original Jail Breaker and Handcuff King; Life, History and Handcuff Secrets of Houdini; Handcuff Tricks Exposed;* and *Houdini, the Adventurous Life of a Versatile Artist.* There are nine examples in the Christopher Collection.

The Right Way to Do Wrong. An Exposé of Successful Criminals. Boston, 1906, published by author.

Editor, publisher, *Conjurers' Monthly Magazine.* New York, September 1906–August 1908.

The Unmasking of Robert-Houdin. New York, Publishers Printing Co., 1908.

The Unmasking of Robert-Houdin Together With a Treatise on Handcuff Secrets. London, George Routledge & Sons, Ltd., 1909.

Mein Training und meine Tricks. Leipzig, Berlin, München, Paris, Grethlein & Co., 1909.

Handcuff Secrets. London, George Routledge & Sons, Ltd., 1910.

The Marvelous Adventures of Houdini, the Justly Celebrated Elusive American. Brooklyn, N. Y., 1917, published by author.

Editor, *M-U-M.* The Society of American Magicians Monthly. New York, 1917–1926.

Miracle Mongers and Their Methods. New York, E. P. Dutton & Co., 1920.

Magical Rope Ties and Escapes. London, Will Goldston, Ltd., 1921.

Mysterious Mr. Yu or Haldane of the Secret Service. New York, 1921, published by author.

Yar, the Primeval Man. New York, 1921, published by author.

Il Mistero di Osiris or the Mystery of the Jewel (Talisman); Mystery Tale of Old Egypt by "Giovanni Deadota." New York, 1921; published by author.

Houdini's Paper Magic. New York, E. P. Dutton & Co., 1922.

Editor, *Elliott's Last Legacy, Secrets of the King of All Kard Kings,* by Dr. James William Elliott. Compiled by Clinton Burgess. New York, Adams Press Print, 1923.

A Magician Among the Spirits. New York, Harper & Brothers, 1924.

Houdini Exposes the Tricks Used by the Boston Medium "Margery.„. . . Also a Complete Exposure of Argamasilla. . . . New York, Adams Press Publishers, 1924.

Editor, "Red Magic." The New York *World* Sunday Supplement (also syndicated as "Home Magic"), 1924–1926.

Houdini Souvenir Program. New York, 1925.

"Conjuring," *Encyclopaedia Britannica,* 13th ed., 1926.

Houdini Souvenir Program Coast to Coast Tour. Season 1926–27. New York, 1926.
Houdini's Book of Magic and Party Pastimes. New York, Stoll & Evans Co., Inc., 1927.
Houdini's Big Little Book of Magic. Racine, Wisc., Whitman Publishing Company, 1927.

In addition to writing hundreds of articles for newspapers, conjuring periodicals, and theatrical journals, Houdini contributed to many magazines: among them, *Collier's, Popular Science, Vanity Fair, Hearst's, Popular Radio, The American Magazine,* and *Weird Tales.*

A Houdini bibliography by Manuel Weltman, listing more than two hundred items, was published in *Genii*, the magic monthly, in October, November, December 1967, and January 1968.

GENERAL WORKS

Abbot, Anthony (Fulton Oursler), *These Are Strange Tales.* Philadelphia, The John C. Winston Company, 1948.

Anonymous, *Secret of the Great Handcuff Trick.* Boston, Mutual Book Company, 1907.

———, *The Davenport Brothers, the World-Renowned Spiritual Mediums.* Boston, William White and Company, 1869.

Bird, J. Malcolm, *"Margery" the Medium.* Boston, Small, Maynard & Co., 1925.

Boston, George L., with Robert Parrish, *Inside Magic.* New York, The Beechhurst Press, 1947.

Cannell, J. C., *The Secrets of Houdini.* London, Hutchinson & Co., Ltd., 1932.

Carrington, Hereward, *The Physical Phenomena of Spiritualism.* Boston, Small, Maynard & Co., 1907.

———, *Handcuff Tricks.* Kansas City, Mo., A. M. Wilson, 1913.

Christopher, Milbourne, *Panorama of Prestidigitators.* New York, The Christopher Collection, 1956.

———, *Panorama of Magic.* New York, Dover Publications, Inc., 1962.

———, *Houdini: The Untold Story.* New York, Thomas Y. Crowell Company, 1969; London, Cassell, 1969.

———, *ESP, Seers & Psychics.* New York, Thomas Y. Crowell Company, 1970.

———, *Seers, Psychics and ESP.* London, Cassell, 1971.

———, *The Illustrated History of Magic.* New York, Thomas Y. Crowell Company, 1973; London, Peter Hale, 1975.

———, *Mediums, Mystics & the Occult.* New York, Thomas Y. Crowell Company, 1975.

Clarke, Sidney W., *The Annals of Conjuring.* London, George Johnson, 1929; also published serially in *The Magic Wand*, 1924–1928.

Clempert, John, *Thrilling Episodes of John Clempert. The Shining Star of the Realms of Mystery.* England, 1909, published by author.

Courtney, Charles, in collaboration with Tom Johnson, *Unlocking Adventure.* New York, Whittlesey House, 1942.

Crandon, L. R. G., *The Margery Mediumship. Unofficial Sittings at the Laboratory of the Society for Psychical Research, London, December 6, 7 and 8, 1929.* Boston, 1930, published by author.

Crawford, W. J., *The Psychic Structures at the Goligher Circle.* London, John M. Watkins, 1921.

Cunningham, Robert, *Cunning "The Jail Breaker." Jail Breaking a Science.* U.S.A., 1907, published by author.

Curry, Paul, *Magician's Magic.* New York, Franklin Watts, Inc., 1965.

Davenport, Reuben Briggs, *The Death-Blow to Spiritualism.* New York, C. W. Dillingham, 1888.

Day, J., *Secrets of the Handcuff Trick.* Birmingham, England, n.d.

Dexter, Will, *This Is Magic.* London, Arco Publications, Ltd., 1958.

Doerr, H. R., *The Secrets of Houdini's Feats Explained.* Philadelphia n.d., published by author.

Doyle, Arthur Conan, *The Edge of the Unknown.* New York, G. P. Putnam's Sons, 1930.

———, *The History of Spiritualism.* (Facsimile of the 1924 edition; two volumes published as one.) New York, Arno Press, 1975.

Dunninger, Joseph, *Houdini's Spirit Exposés*. Ed., Joseph H. Kraus, New York, Experimenter Publishing Co., Inc., 1928.

———, *Inside the Medium's Cabinet*. New York, David Kemp and Company, 1935.

———, *100 Houdini Tricks You Can Do*. New York, Arco Publishing Company, Inc., 1954.

Ernst, Bernard M. L., and Hereward Carrington, *Houdini and Conan Doyle: The Story of a Strange Friendship*. New York, Albert and Charles Boni, Inc., 1932.

Ernst, John, *Escape King: The Story of Harry Houdini*. Englewood Cliffs, N.J., Prentice-Hall, Inc., 1965.

Evans, Henry Ridgely, *The Old and the New Magic*. Chicago, The Open Court Publishing Company, 1906; 2d ed., revised and enlarged, 1909.

———, *Adventures in Magic*. New York, Leo Rullman, 1927.

———, *History of Conjuring and Magic*. Kenton, Ohio, International Brotherhood of Magicians, 1928; new and rev. ed. (abridged). Kenton, Ohio, W. W. Durbin, 1930.

———, *A Master of Modern Magic. The Life and Adventures of Robert-Houdin*. New York, Macoy Publishing Company, 1932.

Fast, Francis R., *The Houdini Messages*. New York, n.d., published by author.

Finger Print Demonstrations by E. E. Dudley, Arthur Goadby, Hereward Carrington. Boston Society for Psychic Research. Bulletin XVIII, October 1932.

Ford, Arthur, in collaboration with Marguerite Harmon Bro, *Nothing So Strange*. New York, Harper & Brothers, 1958.

Fortune Telling, Hearings before the Subcommittee on Judiciary of the Committee on the District of Columbia House of Representatives Sixty-Ninth Congress, First Session, on H.R. 8989, February 26, May 18, 20, and 21, 1924. Washington, Government Printing Office, 1924.

Frikell, Samri (Fulton Oursler), *Spirit Mediums Exposed*. New York, New Metropolitan Fiction, Inc., 1930.

Furst, Arnold, *Great Magic Shows*. Los Angeles, The Genii Publishing Company, 1968.

Gibson, Walter B., *Houdini's Escapes*. New York, Harcourt, Brace & Company, 1930.

———, *Houdini's Magic*. New York, Harcourt, Brace & Company, 1932.

———, *Houdini's Magic and Escapes*. (The two books in one volume.) New York, Blue Ribbon Books, Inc., n.d.

———, and Morris N. Young (eds. and comps.), *Houdini on Magic*. New York, Dover Publications, Inc., 1953.

———, and Morris N. Young. *Houdini's Fabulous Magic*. Philadelphia and New York, Chilton Company, 1961.

———, *The Master Magicians*. Garden City, N.Y., Doubleday & Company, Inc., 1966.

———, *Houdini's Magic and Escapes*. New York, Funk & Wagnalls, 1975. (New introduction by Milbourne Christopher.)

Goldston, Will, *Secrets of Magic*. Liverpool, England, The 'Mahatma' Magical Company, 1903.

———, (ed.), *The Magician Annual 1909–10*. London, A. W. Gamage, Ltd.

———, *Exclusive Magical Secrets*. London, The Magician Ltd., 1912.

———, *Further Exclusive Magical Secrets*. London, Will Goldston, Ltd., 1927.

———, *Sensational Tales of Mystery Men*. London, Will Goldston, Ltd., 1929.

———, *Great Magicians' Tricks*. London, Will Goldston, Ltd., 1931.

———, *A Magician's Swan Song*. London, John Long, Ltd., n.d.

Gresham, William Lindsay, *Houdini, the Man Who Walked Through Walls*. New York, Henry Holt & Company, Inc., 1959.

Hammond, William Elliott, *Houdini Unmasked*. Ca. 1926, published by author.

Hardeen, Theodore (comp.), *Life and History of Hardeen*. Ca. 1926, published by author.

———, *Houdini, His Life and Work in Prose and Picture*. 1927, published by author.

Hugard, Jean, *Houdini's "Unmasking"; Fact vs Fiction*. With an *Introduction and Supplementary Chapter by Milbourne Christopher*. Printed in book form, with a title page dated 1957, as part of *Hugard's Magic Monthly* (Brooklyn), June 1957–January 1959.

Hull, Burling, *The Challenge Handcuff Act*. New York, 1916, published by author.

———, *Thirty-three Rope Ties and Chain Releases*. New York, American Magic Corporation, 1915.

Hunt, Douglas, and Kari Hunt, *The Art of Magic*. New York, Atheneum, 1967.

Kellock, Harold, *Houdini, His Life-Story, by Harold Kellock from the Recollections and Documents of Beatrice Houdini*. New York, Harcourt, Brace & Company, 1928.

Kendall, Lace, *Houdini, Master of Escape*. Philadelphia, Macrae Smith Co., 1960.

Leat, Harry, *Forty Years in and Around Magic*. London, 1923, published by author.

McComas, Henry C., *Ghosts I Have Talked With*. Baltimore, Williams & Wilkins Company, 1935.

McKenzie, J. Hewat, *Spirit Intercourse, Its Theory and Practice*. London, Simpkin, Marshall, Hamilton Kent & Co., Ltd., 1916.

Margery Mediumship, The. Proceedings of the American Society for Psychical Research. New York, 1928, 1933; 3 vols.

Mulholland, John, *Quicker Than the Eye*. Indianapolis, The Bobbs-Merrill Company, 1932.

————, *The Story of Magic*. New York, Loring & Mussey, 1935.

————, *Beware Familiar Spirits*. New York, Charles Scribner's Sons, 1938.

Murchison, Carl (ed.), *The Case For and Against Psychical Belief*. Worcester, Mass., Clark University, 1927.

Pressing, R. G. (comp.), *Houdini Unmasked*. Lily Dale, N.Y., *Dale News*, 1947.

Rauscher, William V., *The Spiritual Frontier*. Garden City, New York, Doubleday & Company Inc., 1975.

Reeve, Arthur B., and John W. Grey, *The Master Mystery from Scenarios*. New York, Grosset & Dunlap, 1919.

Richardson, Mark, . . . L. R. G. Crandon, *Margery, Harvard, Veritas: A Study in Psychics*. Boston, Blanchard Printing., 1925.

Rinn, Joseph F., *Sixty Years of Psychical Research*. New York, The Truth Seeker Company, 1950.

Robert-Houdin, Jean Eugène, *Memoirs of Robert-Houdin, King of the Conjurers*. New Introduction and Notes by Milbourne Christopher. New York, Dover Publications, Inc., 1964.

Sardina, Maurice, *Where Houdini Was Wrong*. Tr. and ed. with Notes by Victor Farelli. London, George Armstrong, 1950.

Seldow, Michel, *Les Illusionnistes et Leur Secrets*. Paris, Librairie Arthème Fayard, 1959.

Severn, Bill, *Magic and Magicians*. New York, David McKay Company, Inc., 1958.

Sharpe, S. H., *Introducing Houdini versus Robert-Houdin: The Whole Truth*. Reighton, England, 1955, published by author.

Spraggett, Allen, with William V. Rauscher, *Arthur Ford: The Man Who Talked with the Dead*. New York, New American Library, 1973.

Stanyon, Ellis, *Great Handcuff Secrets*. London, Stanyon & Co., 1904.

Tietze, Thomas, *Margery*. New York, Harper & Row, 1973.

Truesdell, John W., *The Bottom Facts Concerning the Science of Spiritualism*. New York, G. W. Carleton & Co., 1883.

Williams, Beryl, and Samuel Epstein, *The Great Houdini*. New York, Julian Messner, Inc., 1950.

Wilsmann, Aloys Christof, *Die Zersägte Jungfrau*. Berlin, Verlag Scherl, 1938.

INDEX